For Grade

3

Parent/Teacher Edition

Write on Target

Using Graphic Organizers to Improve Writing Skills

D1455837

Written By:
Yolande F. Grizinski, Ed.D.
Leslie Holzhauser-Peters, MS, CCC-SP

Show What You Know
Publishing

Published By:
Show What You Know® Publishing
A Division of Englefield & Associates, Inc.
P.O. Box 341348
Columbus, OH 43234-1348
614-764-1211

www.showwhatyouknowpublishing.com

Printed in the United States of America
07 06 05   20 19 18 17 16 15 14 13 12 11 10 9 8 7 6 5 4 3 2 1

ISBN: 1-59230-150-9

About the Authors

Yolande F. Grizinski received a Bachelor's degree from Miami University, a Master's degree from Wright State University, and a Doctor of Education from the University of Cincinnati. She has worked in public education for thirty years as a curriculum consultant in the areas of language arts with a focus on writing assessment. She is currently the Assistant Superintendent of the Warren County Educational Service Center in Lebanon, Ohio.

Leslie Holzhauser-Peters holds a Bachelor's degree from the University of Cincinnati and Master's degree from Miami University. She has twenty-seven years of experience working in public schools in Special Education and as a Speech-language pathologist, as a Supervisor, and currently as a Curriculum Consultant. Her areas of expertise are language, literacy, and intervention.

The authors met at the Warren County Educational Service Center in Lebanon, Ohio. There they developed and implemented a host of language arts initiatives including a large-scale writing assessment. They have given numerous presentations on the five communication processes and Ohio's proficiencies.

Acknowledgements

Show What You Know® Publishing acknowledges the following for their efforts in making this assessment material available for students, parents, and teachers.

Cindi Englefield, President/Publisher
Eloise Boehm-Sasala, Vice President/Managing Editor
Lainie Burke Rosenthal, Project Editor/Graphic Designer
Erin McDonald, Project Editor
Christine Filippetti, Project Editor
Jill Borish, Project Editor
Charles V. Jackson, Project Editor
Heather Holliday, Project Editor
Jennifer Harney, Illustrator/Cover Designer

© 2005 Englefield & Associates, Inc.

Table of Contents

Foreword

We are fortunate to have worked with many wonderful educators and students in the years before writing this book. For the past fifteen years, we have examined over 40,000 student papers that were responses to prompts that provided students with on-demand writing tasks.

In our work, we have observed that many students have the ideas and motivation to complete the writing tasks asked of them but are unable to demonstrate appropriate writing skills. We have learned, through many years of large-scale writing assessment, that students often fall short in the organization of their thoughts and ideas. It was apparent in many cases that students did not have specific or organized structures "inside their heads" to plan their writing. As a result, their writing did not address the mode, was disorganized, shifted among purposes, and had weak endings. To improve students' organizational skills, we developed a graphic organizer for each of the 11 modes of writing. We tied each mode to one of five communication processes— narration, description, directions, explanation, and persuasion.

The model lesson format found in this book was demonstrated to classroom teachers with significant numbers of students at risk. These teachers used the model lesson format, modeling technique, and graphic organizers with their "at risk" students. After working for seven to eight months, these teachers found that their students' writing scores were the best in the building! Critical to this success was the ability of the classroom teacher to model the use of the graphic organizers over and over again, using clear examples for each mode of writing as a model.

Included in this book are descriptions of the five communication processes and 11 modes of writing, 22 model lessons, 22 prompts written with a purpose and an audience, 11 graphic organizers, student checklists, additional writing prompts, and a description of where students typically break down in the writing process.

The tools found in this book will serve students well as they work to improve their writing skills.

Introduction

What are Graphic Organizers?

Graphic organizers provide students with an organizational framework to help them plan their thinking and organize their thoughts. The use of graphic organizers increases the reader's and writer's comprehension of the text by providing a map to:

- find connections,

- organize large amounts of information,

- brainstorm ideas, and

- make decisions.

Each graphic organizer in this program shows the key parts of the communication process and the relationship of these parts to the whole.

The greatest challenge some students face is their ability to organize their writing into an orderly framework that is understood by the reader. In both reading and writing, students are asked to interpret and comprehend meaning. The graphic organizer is a tool that can assist students during the reading and writing process. While reading with the graphic organizer, students can increase their comprehension by using the graphic organizer to trace the organization of the reading selection. While writing with the graphic organizer, the students can place their own ideas and thoughts into a structure that fits the purpose of the prompt.

Using Graphic Organizers to Succeed

This book provides third-grade classroom teachers with a lesson plan framework for teaching writing skills to promote student success.

Five specific communication processes (narration, description, directions, explanation, and persuasion) have been selected and paired with specific graphic organizers for instructional use.

The five communication processes can be further broken down into eleven writing modes. (A description of each mode can be found in Preface One.) In order for students to be successful writers, they must be skillful in responding to eleven different types (modes) of writing.

Successful Results with Graphic Organizers

We have seen significant improvement when graphic organizers were used in both regular classroom instruction and large-scale, on-demand writing assessments. Students are able to understand information, organize their thoughts, and stay focused on their writing.

When the appropriate graphic organizer is used, teachers are able to trace a student's thinking during the planning stage of writing. After using the graphic organizer, we see in students' work an improved organizational structure with a clear beginning, middle, and end. Students are able to write to the purpose of the mode even when the students' final products are not fully developed. Teachers can see where students break down in the writing process and plan intervention.

Targeted Areas to Improve

Through our experiences in scoring and reflecting on students' writing samples, we recognize there is a significant need to improve student writing content, organization, and clarity in addressing a prompt. We observed that student papers often contained problems with:

- no clear ending or sense of closure;

- shifts among the communication processes (for example, students moved between personal experience narrative and directions); and/or

- ideas were presented randomly with no sequence or organization.

Holistic Scores Improve

We could see the development of wonderful ideas on topics by students when graphic organizers were presented. We found that their holistic scores improved with significant gains in content and organization when:

1. The same lesson plan framework was used for any writing task.

2. The graphic organizer was tailored to match the purpose of the writing prompt.

3. The same set of graphic organizers was used over and over again so that students developed consistency when writing to the basic communication processes.

Ways to Use *Write on Target* in Your Writing Program

Primary Purpose

The primary purpose of this book is to enable students to understand the unique features of each of the five communication processes (narration, description, directions, explanation, and persuasion) and to practice eleven modes of writing.

Write on Target has graphic organizers that match eleven modes of writing. Each graphic organizer was developed to incorporate those components of the writing mode that make it unique and different from the others. The goal in having students use the graphic organizers is to provide them with an organizational framework that allows them to learn and integrate the characteristics and components of each mode. The goal is to use the same graphic organizer any time the student is to write or speak using that particular mode. If students are asked to use a different graphic organizer each time they write or speak, the purpose is defeated.

Students may not understand how to use graphic organizers initially. They often use the graphic organizers to write out their entire paper rather than as a planning guide.

Guidelines for Using the Graphic Organizer

1. Model the use of the graphic organizer by thinking through the planning of a written piece.

2. Model the completion of the graphic organizer by inserting a word, phrase, picture, or abbreviation in each box. This modeling process needs to occur over and over again.

3. Explain to students the purpose of the graphic organizer. Students need to know that their time and energy should be reserved for writing their own piece.

4. Model how to transfer thoughts organized on the graphic organizer into a written piece.

5. Share the rubrics used for scoring with the students. Student models of the various rubric levels (4, 3, 2, 1, 0) should be shared regularly with students.

In addition, *Write on Target* can be used in the following ways:

1. as a major component of a **year-long writing program**. Students would complete two prompts for each of the eleven modes in grade three.

2. as a **pre- or post-assessment** for each of the eleven modes of writing for a particular grade level.

3. as an **assessment portfolio** that would move with each student from grade three to grade four.

4. as a **bank of prompts** that supports regular classroom instruction.

5. as support for concentrated **standardized test preparation** programs.

6. as a **summer school writing program** or as part of an **intervention program**.

7. as **"on-demand" writing tasks** for individual practice.

Ways to Use *Write on Target* in Your Reading Program

In addition to the writing process, graphic organizers can be used to assist comprehension during the reading process. The graphic organizers will assist students in covering the following skills to improve reading comprehension:

1. **Comprehend Fiction and Nonfiction Selections**

   - to assess what a student knows about a topic (prior knowledge)

   - to organize ideas in reading materials

   - to gain an understanding of the structure of a specific communication process (purpose)

   - to guide and focus students' thinking during class discussion of student writing or reading materials

2. **Interpret Fiction and Nonfiction Selections**

   - to facilitate text comprehension by making new connections

   - to see how things are related

   - to organize personal reactions, thoughts, and feelings

   - to create original products to fit a specific communication process (purpose)

Modes of Writing

What Writing Skills Should Third Graders Have?

By the time students reach third grade, they are expected to write for a variety of purposes and to a variety of audiences. These eleven modes of writing prepare students to write for school success, and they prepare them for the skills of life.

Eleven Modes of Writing:

1. **Fictional narrative** – a piece of writing that has a title, named characters, and events that detail what happens. A fictional narrative establishes an inferred or explicit problem. It has a beginning, a middle, and an end. A fictional narrative is a made-up story that could appear to be true to the reader.

2. **Personal experience narrative** – a piece of writing that has a title and a beginning, a middle, and an end. It is a story based on the student's own life experiences, and it discusses who was there, when it happened, and where it happened. A personal experience narrative has to be believable but does not have to be true.

3. **Retelling** – a piece of writing that starts with the beginning of the story and retells the story in the same order as the original. A retelling is written with a beginning, a middle, and an end. It includes characters that are in the story and uses details from the story. A retelling is written in the student's own words and does not include additional details that were not part of the original story.

4. **Journal** – a piece of writing that includes a date and a description of the writer's feelings, or the sights, sounds, events, and people the writer has encountered. Often, the audience is the writer.

5. **Descriptive letter** – a piece of writing that has a specific form which includes a greeting, a body, and a closing. A letter addresses a specific audience and establishes a written connection with that audience.

Eleven Modes of Writing (continued):

6. **Directions** – a piece of writing that explains how to do something or how to go somewhere. It clearly describes the materials that are needed to complete the task and uses step-by-step order. Directions may be written in paragraph form or line-by-line. A starting point and and ending point are included.

7. **Invitation** – a piece of writing that can be in letter format. An invitation includes the purpose of the invitation, who is writing the invitation, who is being invited, where and when the event takes place, and any other important information.

8. **Thank-you note** – a piece of writing that is written in the form of a letter and includes a greeting, a body, a closing, and a signature. A thank-you note explains what the writer is thankful for and why.

9. **Summary** – a piece of writing identifying what the text selection is about. A summary states the main ideas of the text selection. It does not include information that is not important. A summary has fewer details than a retelling.

10. **Informational report** – a piece of nonfiction writing that is based on researched facts, but is written in the student's own words. It is presented in an organized format with a beginning, a middle, and an end. It can cover a wide variety of topics. The purpose of an informational piece of writing is to inform the reader about what the author has learned.

11. **Letter to the editor** – a piece of writing that is written in the form of a letter and includes a date, a greeting, a body, a closing, and a signature. A letter to the editor expresses the writer's opinion and why it is important by using facts, examples, or reasons. It also states what the writer would like to see happen.

Using Graphic Organizers

The Model Lesson

There are four major components key to any good lesson that incorporates graphic organizers. These four components include:

1. **Prior Knowledge** – to determine the student's prior knowledge about the topic, purpose, or task of the lesson.

2. **Model** – to model the use of the graphic organizer through class discussion with the thinking process modeled aloud as the organizer is completed.

3. **Guided Practice** – to provide guided practice by presenting a task for students to complete that matches the purpose of the graphic organizer you want to teach.

4. **Independent Practice** – to provide independent practice so students are provided with on-demand writing tasks that are organized according to the purpose.

Defining Each Component of the Model Lesson

I.   Determining Prior Knowledge of Students

Students must make personal connections with the purpose of the material being presented. Establishing a student's familiarity with the material is important for interpreting and comprehending meaning and ultimately retaining information. The following questions can be used with any lesson to tap into prior knowledge of the whole class or for an individual student:

1. What do you know about _____? (The student response provides the teacher with an assessment of what he or she knows prior to the lesson.)

2. Where do you see this in your life? (The student response helps to establish the importance of the task for now and for the future.)

Both of these questions show how students are connected with the material. This process is important for the retention of information. Students need to make connections themselves.

Sample Questions to Tap Prior Knowledge:

- Does anyone know what a narrative is?

- What do we know about narratives?

- What are some parts of a narrative?

- What is the narrative's purpose? or audience?

- Who reads or writes narratives?

- Where do you see narratives every day?

- What does personal mean?

- What is a personal narrative?

II.   Modeling

Modeling or demonstrating the thinking process for the use of the selected graphic organizer is an important component of any lesson. Modeling must be done frequently because it is the part of the lesson by which students construct meaning.

There are two types of modeling:

1. Demonstrating the thinking process used in completing a graphic organizer.

2. Providing samples of both acceptable and unacceptable writing keyed to the holistic scoring rubric. (The scoring rubric can be found on page 11.)

Both types of modeling must be done frequently. Time is well spent during the modeling phase of the lesson. Modeling clarifies the task and enables the student to internalize the standard.

The model needs to match the purpose of the writing task the students will complete. Written models can be obtained from a variety of sources (see chart on the next page). Once you become aware of the writing modes, you and your students will be able to select written models from a variety of sources:

- newspapers

- trade books

- textbooks

- student generated models*

---

*   *Over time, develop a bank of students' responses that are good examples of the different types of writing modes; include different levels of the scoring rubric.*

The Five Communication Processes
Matched with Eleven Writing Modes

Communication Process	Writing Modes	Sources of Modes
Narrative	Fictional Narratives	magazines, trade books, literature-based reading series
	Personal Experience Narratives	newspapers, diaries, journals
	Retellings	personal conversations, police and accident reports, testimonials
Descriptive*	Journals	diaries, journals, science reports, advertisements
	Letters	personal correspondence, published documents
Directions	Directions	recipes, stage directions, maps
	Invitations	weddings, birthdays, parties, formal and informal formats
Explanation	Informational Reports	business reports, science and social studies text books, newspapers, and magazines
	Summaries	movie reviews, book jackets, encyclopedia
	Thank-You Notes	personal correspondence
Persuasion	Letters to the Editor	letter to the editor of a newspaper or magazine

*   *Note: The ability to describe is an important skill embedded in many of the communication processes and writing modes.*

III.   Guided Practice

During guided practice, the teacher should provide various levels of support to students as needed.

Provide a task for students to complete that matches what you want to teach in the most authentic way possible. For example, have students write a persuasive letter to the editor of the newspaper regarding an issue facing the school or community, or ask students to write a set of directions to be followed.

After considerable guided practice, provide students with many opportunities to engage in independent practice with "on-demand" writing prompts. Sample prompts are included at the end of each chapter of this book.

IV.   Independent Practice

Independent practice is an "on-demand" task that provides students with a test-like writing experience. During independent practice, students should be given a graphic organizer, a writing prompt with a specific purpose, a writing model (optional), lined paper, and a writing checklist. It is important that teachers provide enough time for students to complete the writing task.

During independent practice, no teacher or peer assistance should be provided to students. No reference materials can be used. Independent practice is different from lessons that take students through all stages of the writing process. These student papers are considered rough drafts and scored accordingly with the scoring rubric. It is critical that students be provided with this type of task on many occasions throughout the school year.

The "on-demand" writing task is designed so that students can choose to use either print or cursive formats. The students should choose the format that is most comfortable to them. Every attempt should be made to determine the meaning and content of each student's paper. Legibility issues should be minimized whenever possible.

After the students have completed this type of independent practice, it is the role of the teacher to return to the model lesson and cycle through the lesson again before the next independent practice is presented to the class.

Rubric for Holistic Scoring of Student Writing

The scoring of papers is designed to focus on the most important features of a piece of writing. The writer's ability to transmit meaning to the reader by writing to the purpose with strong organization is considered most important and given most value.

Weighting of Writing Features

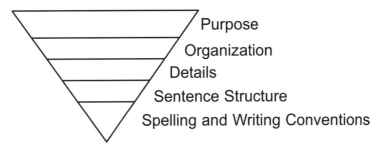

Purpose
Organization
Details
Sentence Structure
Spelling and Writing Conventions

A **4-point** response clearly addresses the topic and purpose. It has organized ideas with a logical beginning, middle, and end. It includes supporting details. It uses language effectively with a variety of words and sentence patterns. The beginning of sentences are capitalized, and the ends of sentences are appropriately punctuated. Most commonly used words are spelled correctly. It attempts to show a personal style and sense of audience.

A **3-point** response addresses the topic and purpose. It has organized ideas with a mostly logical beginning, middle, and end. It includes supporting details. It attempts to use a variety of words and sentence patterns. The beginning of sentences are capitalized, and the ends of sentences are appropriately punctuated. Most commonly used words are spelled correctly.

A **2-point** response attempts to address the topic and purpose. It has organized ideas with an undeveloped beginning, middle, or end (often doesn't include ending or sense of closure). It uses few details and may include extraneous information that is unrelated to the topic. The beginning of most sentences are capitalized, and the ends of most sentences are correctly punctuated. Some commonly used words are spelled correctly (spelling errors may interfere with the message).

A **1-point** response minimally addresses the topic and purpose. It shows little or no organizational pattern. It presents limited details. It uses language or sentence patterns that greatly interfere with meaning. It uses beginning capitalization and ending punctuation incorrectly. It contains so many spelling errors that the meaning of the paper is obscured.

An **unscorable** response is a paper that does not fit into any of the above categories. These individual cases may include papers that are illegible, off topic, written in a language other than English, or those that are blank.

Model Lesson: Putting It All Together, Step-by-Step

Writing activities for each writing mode are arranged step-by-step in the Parent/Teacher Edition and Student Workbook. The following steps are derived from the four components of the Model Lesson. Each time you teach a lesson, you may want to refer to these steps. This model lesson guide is directly matched to the writing activities in the chapters that follow.

Prior Knowledge

Before you begin, ask students, "What do you know about (*insert one of the writing modes, e.g., fictional narrative*)? Where have you seen this in your life?"

Model

Step 1:

- Introduce a model text selection that is typical of the writing mode you are describing.

- Read the model and highlight its features.

- Show the graphic organizer that corresponds to the writing mode. (Full size graphic organizers can be found throughout the Student Workbook.)

- Use the model text selection to complete the graphic organizer.

- Explain how the graphic organizer should be used by completing the graphic organizer on an overhead, or by providing each student with a personal copy.

- As a class, demonstrate the completion of the graphic organizer using a think aloud technique.

Step 2:

Discuss the characteristics of the communication process you are introducing.

                   © 2005 Englefield & Associates, Inc.

Model Lesson: Putting It All Together, Step-by-Step

Guided Practice

Step 3:

Introduce the prompt students will be addressing as well as the appropriate graphic organizer. Students should think about how they will address the prompt.

Step 4:

Students will complete the graphic organizer based on the prompt. The graphic organizer will help students arrange their thoughts.

Step 5:

Each student will complete the writing activity based on the prompt and the information he or she has organized with the graphic organizer.

Step 6:

The checklist provided in this section shows what a student's best paper must include. Students should use this checklist as a guideline for their responses.

Independent Practice

Once students have completed the six steps, they are ready for independent practice. Provide students with on-demand writing tasks. Refer to the additional prompts, specific to each writing mode, found at the end of each chapter of this book. (For more information on independent practice, refer to Section IV on page 10 of this chapter.)

The final step is scoring the student papers. Score the papers based on the scoring rubric. Students should become familiar with the standards of the four-point rubric.

Designing Your Own Writing Prompts

Guidelines to Consider

1. **A clear purpose must be specified.** Choose the writing mode you want to test and tell the students what they are expected to do. Use words such as "describe," "persuade," or "retell" in the directions. Keep the prompt as simple as possible. Prompts should be comprised of words your students can easily read and understand. The writing test should not become a reading test.

2. **The audience should be indicated.** The audience should be a person or a group the students would feel comfortable addressing. Often for the purposes of the writing assessment, teacher scorers are the audience.

3. **Students should have a solid prior knowledge base about the topic before they begin writing.** The subject matter of the writing prompt should be within the realm of each student's experience and should not involve emotionally charged issues that would distract from the writing task. For example, not all students have visited Canada. Asking students to describe the landscape of Canada would be unfair to those students who have not experienced the Canadian landscape firsthand. An alternative might be to ask students to describe their idea of a beautiful landscape.

4. **The evaluation criteria and prompt checklist should be reviewed with students before administering the on-demand writing task.** The scoring rubric should not be a mystery to the students. Students need to develop a clear understanding of the standard and scoring procedures. We have found that students become excellent scorers when trained to use the rubric.

The Narrative Communication Process

(Fictional Narrative, Personal Experience Narrative, and Retelling)

The purposes of this chapter include:

1 Showing how the narrative communication process links to the writing modes.

2 Discussing the purpose and features of a personal experience narrative, a fictional narrative, and a retelling.

3 Offering teaching tips on where students break down in the narrative process.

4 Providing ideas for the development of additional writing prompts for the fictional narrative, personal experience narrative, and retelling.

> The following teaching tools are provided for a **fictional narrative**, a **personal experience narrative**, and a **retelling**: graphic organizers, two writing prompts, and student checklists.

What is the Narrative Communication Process?

The purpose of a narrative is to tell a story. A fictional narrative is a made-up story. A personal narrative is an account of an event that has happened or could have happened to the writer in real life. A retelling recounts a story with the same sequence of events and details that appear in the original version.

Features of a Fictional Narrative

- Is a made-up story that has a central problem

Features of a Personal Experience Narrative

- Is typically told in the first person ("I")

- Focuses on an event that has or could have happened to the writer in real life

Features of a Retelling

- Restates the story

- Does not add details based on the writer's personal perceptions or opinions

- Is told in the writer's own words; it is not copied

Correlation of Narrative Communication to the Writing Modes

Fictional narrative – a piece of writing that has a title, named characters, and events that detail what happens. A fictional narrative establishes an inferred or explicit problem. It has a beginning, a middle, and an end. A fictional narrative is a made up story that could appear to be true to the reader.

Personal experience narrative – a piece of writing that has a title, a beginning, a middle, and an end. It is a story based on the student's own life experiences, and it discusses who was there, when it happened, and where it happened. A personal experience narrative has to be believable but does not have to be true.

Retelling – a piece of writing that starts with the beginning of the story and retells the story in the same order as the original. A retelling is written with a beginning, a middle, and an end. It includes characters that are in the story and uses details from the story. A retelling is written in the student's own words and does not include additional details that were not part of the original story.

Teaching Tips: Where Students Break Down in the Narrative Communication Process

- Students write the story as they would tell it verbally, so it is not organized in a sequential fashion.

- Students make assumptions that the reader has had the same experience. Students leave out essential information for the reader.

- Students include too much information which takes away from the storyline.

- Students do not stay with the purpose.

- Students confuse personal experience narrative with fictional narrative. A personal experience narrative should include an experience that could or did happen.

- Students write a summary of the story rather than a retelling.

- Students' retellings do not have beginnings, middles, or ends. Students often begin the retelling in the middle of the story and/or leave out major parts of the story.

- Students add details to a retelling that are based on their own perceptions or opinions.

Student Writing Activity 1: Fictional Narrative

Write on Target for Grade 3

Step

1

Follow along as the fictional narrative "Finding a Name" is read aloud.

Finding a Name

It was almost time for the store to close when in came a little girl and her father. They stood around the glass enclosure talking and pointing for a long time. "Daddy," she said "Look at the black one. Can we buy him?"

Her father replied, "Are you sure that's the one you want, Katie?"

"Oh yes!" she exclaimed "I think he is beautiful." Then one of the creatures was quickly scooped up and put in a cardboard box. Katie was so happy as she carried the box out to the car. She could hear the creature moving around inside. When she put the box on the seat of the car, it looked like the box was moving on its own—as if it were magic.

When they arrived at home, Katie hurried up to her room being careful to protect the treasure in the box. She placed the box into the glass container on the table next to her bed and slowly opened the box. Out shot her new pet into the wood shavings that he quickly piled into a cozy nest. He began to run in and out of the paper towel tube and then onto the wheel. Katie had trouble sleeping that night because the squeaking of the wheel going round and round seemed to go on all night.

A few nights later, Katie awoke from a sound sleep because she didn't hear the squeaky wheel. She looked over at the table and into the cage, but it was empty. She jumped out of her bed screaming "Dad, my gerbil is gone!" She and her father immediately began to search the house.

After about fifteen minutes, Katie heard her father say, "I found him, Katie. He was under the couch." Then Katie and her father proceeded to put the gerbil back into his cage. Katie's father said, "Well, Katie, it looks like we need to get a top for this cage. Your gerbil is a clever little guy."

Katie replied, "He is clever, Dad. That gives me an idea for his name. I think I will call him Wiley."

"That sounds like a good name," her father said. Katie's father kissed her good night. Katie and her father then went to sleep, but not Wiley. He was back to running in the wheel for the rest of the night.

Read the passage aloud. Students should follow along in their books. Then, students should complete the graphic organizer and the writing activity using the prompt on Student Workbook page 3.

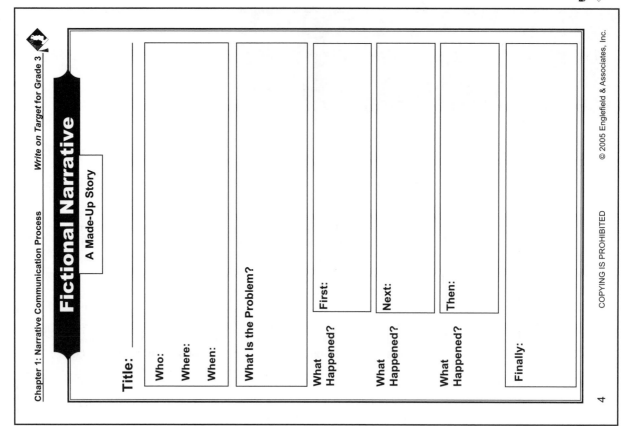

Fictional Narrative
A Made-Up Story

Title: _____

Who:

Where:

When:

What Is the Problem?

What Happened?   First:

What Happened?   Next:

What Happened?   Then:

Finally:

4

Step 2

There are several things to keep in mind as you plan and write your own fictional narrative. Remember, a good fictional narrative has the following parts:

- a title that fits the story
- a character or characters you can picture in your mind
- a problem that a character needs to solve
- a beginning, a middle, and an end (think about what happens first, next, then, and finally)

Step 3

Use the following prompt to complete the prewriting and writing activities:

> Sometimes, people want to go to sleep, but no matter what they do, they just can't fall asleep. Write a fictional narrative about a person who can't get to sleep no matter what he or she does. Write about what is keeping the person awake. Maybe it is what the person is sleeping on or where the person is sleeping. Is it a light, a noise, or a feeling that is keeping this person awake? You decide.

Step 4

Complete the graphic organizer on the next page as your prewriting activity. Use your graphic organizer to help you think through your fictional narrative.

3

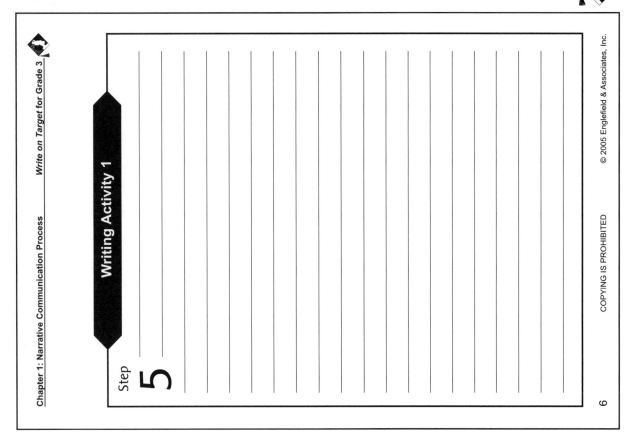

Writing Activity 1

Step 5

6

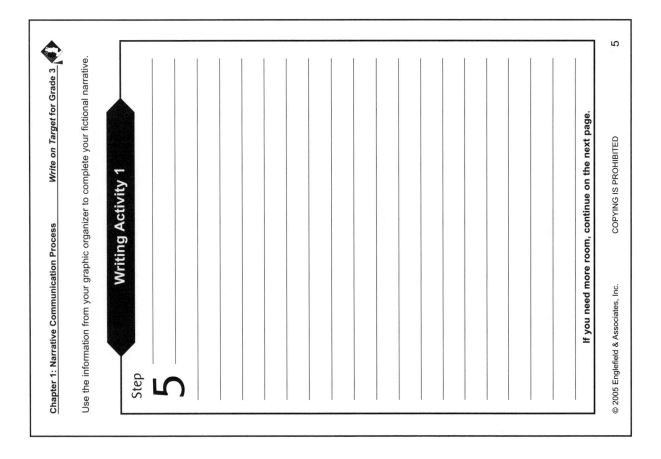

Use the information from your graphic organizer to complete your fictional narrative.

Writing Activity 1

Step 5

If you need more room, continue on the next page.

5

Notes on Student Responses

Step 6

The checklist shows what your best fictional narrative must include. Use the checklist below to review your work.

Checklist for Writing Activity 1

☐ My story has a title.

☐ My characters have names.

☐ My story tells about a person who is having trouble falling asleep.

☐ My story gives details about why the person can't fall asleep.

☐ My story has a beginning, middle, and end.

☐ I try to spell words correctly without using any help.

☐ I use interesting words.

☐ My sentences end with a period, an exclamation point, or a question mark.

☐ My sentences and proper names begin with a capital letter.

☐ I have written my story so the reader can read my print or cursive writing.

Student Writing Activity 2: Fictional Narrative

Step

1

Follow along as the fictional narrative "The Big Lion" is read aloud.

The Big Lion

Danny smelled the soft pretzels, funnel cakes, and fudge when he entered the Queensgate Amusement Park. His father stopped by the ice cream stand and bought Dan his favorite treat—a chocolate-covered vanilla ice cream cone. Danny bit into the chocolate and looked at his father, "Do you think this is the year? Am I big enough?" Just as he asked the question, he saw it. The Big Lion—one of the largest roller coasters he had ever seen.

Danny stood in line for what seemed like forever to see if he was tall enough to ride the roaring, soaring coaster. Finally, he was next. The man at the gate carefully measured him with the stick next to the sign in all capital letters that read: YOU HAVE TO BE THIS TALL TO RIDE THIS RIDE. "Yes, you are a couple of inches over the limit. Watch your step and enter the car slowly."

Danny heard the car screech to a stop. He could hear the screams of the other riders as they traveled the bends and turns of the giant coaster. He entered the car all by himself. He put on the seat belt and carefully placed the iron rail down over his legs. He took a deep breath as the workers checked his belts and doors.

Finally, his car made its way up the first hill as Danny prepared for the ride of his life. He took a deep breath. He was finally ready for the Big Lion!

8   COPYING IS PROHIBITED   © 2005 Englefield & Associates, Inc.

Read the passage aloud. Students should follow along in their books. Then, students should complete the graphic organizer and the writing activity using the prompt on Student Workbook page 9.

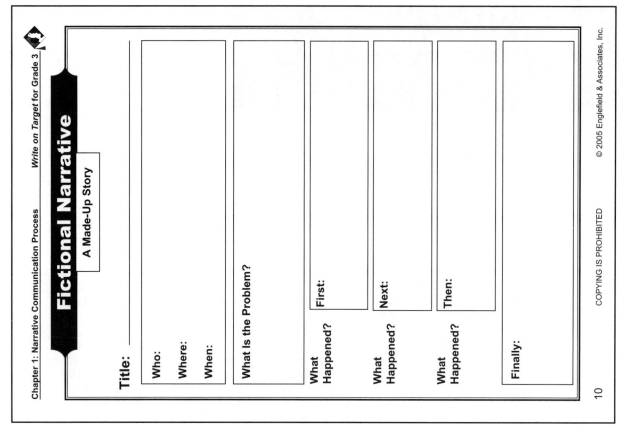

Fictional Narrative
A Made-Up Story

Title: _____

Who:

Where:

When:

What Is the Problem?

What Happened? | First:

What Happened? | Next:

What Happened? | Then:

Finally:

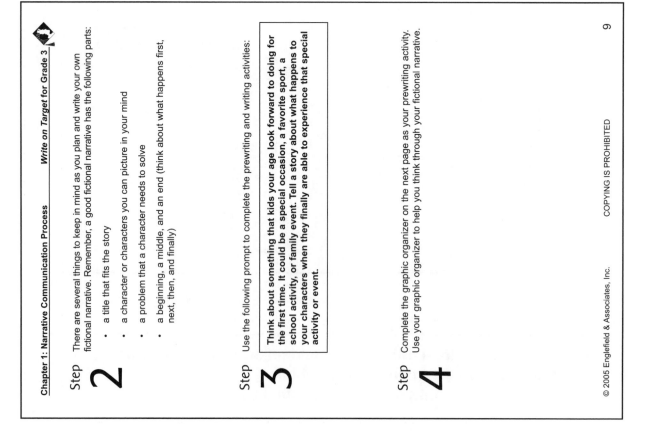

Step 2

There are several things to keep in mind as you plan and write your own fictional narrative. Remember, a good fictional narrative has the following parts:

- a title that fits the story
- a character or characters you can picture in your mind
- a problem that a character needs to solve
- a beginning, a middle, and an end (think about what happens first, next, then, and finally)

Step 3

Use the following prompt to complete the prewriting and writing activities:

> Think about something that kids your age look forward to doing for the first time. It could be a special occasion, a favorite sport, a school activity, or family event. Tell a story about what happens to your characters when they finally are able to experience that special activity or event.

Step 4

Complete the graphic organizer on the next page as your prewriting activity. Use your graphic organizer to help you think through your fictional narrative.

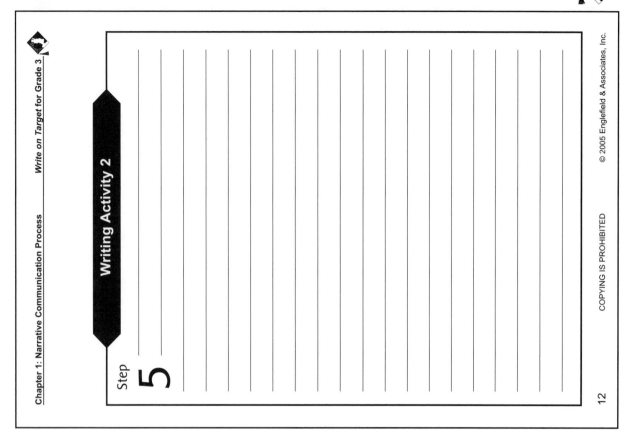

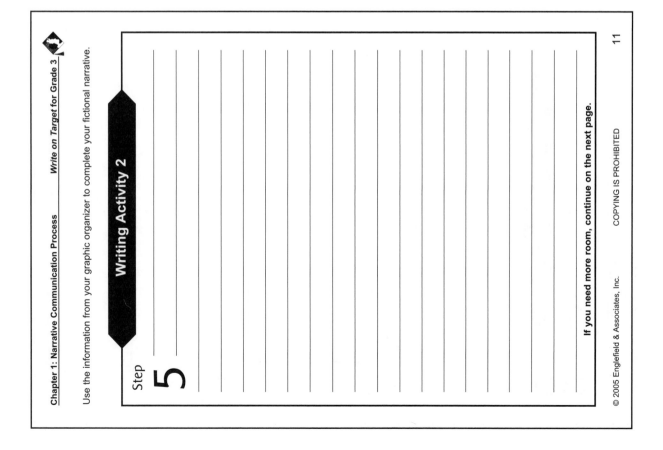

Notes on Student Responses

Step 6

The checklist shows what your best fictional narrative must include. Use the checklist below to review your work.

Checklist for Writing Activity 2

☐ My story has a title.

☐ My characters have names.

☐ My story tells what the special activity or event is.

☐ My story gives details about the activity or event.

☐ My story has a beginning, middle, and end.

☐ I try to spell words correctly without using any help.

☐ I use interesting words.

☐ My sentences end with a period, an exclamation point, or a question mark.

☐ My sentences and proper names begin with a capital letter.

☐ I have written my story so the reader can read my print or cursive writing.

Student Writing Activity 3: Personal Experience Narrative

Write on Target for Grade 3

Step **1**

Follow along as the personal experience narrative "A Happy Memory" is read aloud.

A Happy Memory

We were so excited to arrive at the hotel after sitting in the car for hours. As we unloaded our luggage, my cousins and I discovered our hotel rooms were on the third floor and the hotel had an elevator! We explored for the first few hours, taking the elevator from floor to floor. We poked the buttons and took new guests that arrived to their floor. Our elevator fun had only just begun when our parents decided we were not the welcoming committee. It seemed our assistance was not appreciated by everyone. It was great fun that had to end, so we had to find new entertainment.

My cousins and I went back to my family's room and sat on the chairs on the balcony outside our glass door. As we looked over the railing, we could look down and see people sitting on a wooden dock. They were holding fishing poles, hoping to catch a big one. My cousin ran into our room and returned to the balcony with a bucket of ice. He proceeded to throw a piece of ice over the railing. He quickly sat down, looking as if he hadn't done anything. He did this several times and we began to hear excitement on the dock below.

"Hey, I think you got one," we heard. I looked down at the people fishing and looked at my cousin, trying to figure out what had happened.

I began to smile when I realized that each time he threw an ice cube into the water, it made a little splash. When the people fishing heard the splash, they got excited thinking the splash was made by a fish swimming near their fishing poles. I looked in my cousin's dancing brown eyes, and we began to laugh. Now when I think about that vacation, it brings a smile to my face to think of my cousin and the ice cubes.

14   COPYING IS PROHIBITED   © 2005 Englefield & Associates, Inc.

Read the passage aloud. Students should follow along in their books. Then, students should complete the graphic organizer and the writing activity using the prompt on Student Workbook page 15.

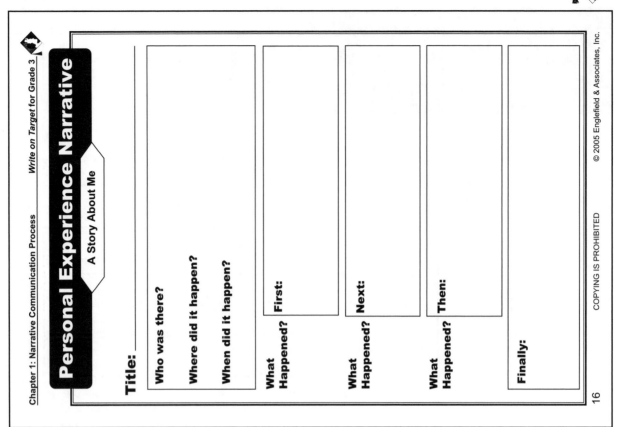

Personal Experience Narrative
A Story About Me

Title: _____

Who was there?

Where did it happen?

When did it happen?

What Happened?   **First:**

What Happened?   **Next:**

What Happened?   **Then:**

Finally:

Step 2

There are several things to keep in mind as you plan and write your own personal experience narrative. Write about something that could or did happen to you in your life. The prewriting graphic organizer will help you get ideas for your story. Remember, a good personal experience narrative has the following parts:

- a title that fits the story

- people you know, or events, special times, and memories that did or could have happened to you in real life

- a beginning, a middle, and an end (think about what happens first, next, then, and finally)

Step 3

Use the following prompt to complete the prewriting and writing activities:

> **You don't always get to do want you want. Write a personal experience narrative about a time you were made to go somewhere or do something, but it turned out to be a good experience. Tell what happened to make it a good experience.**

Step 4

Complete the graphic organizer on the next page as your prewriting activity. Use your graphic organizer to help you think through your personal experience narrative.

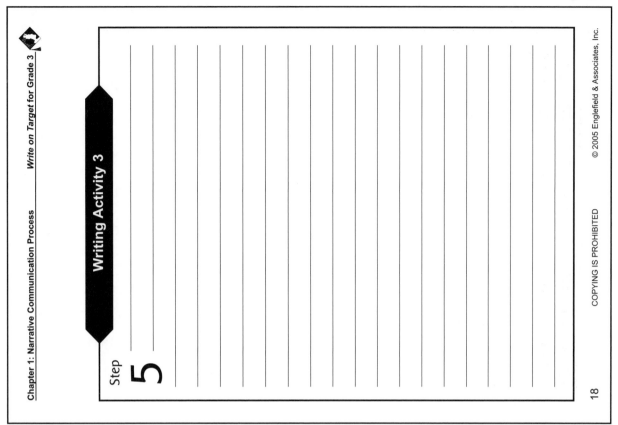

Writing Activity 3

Step 5

18

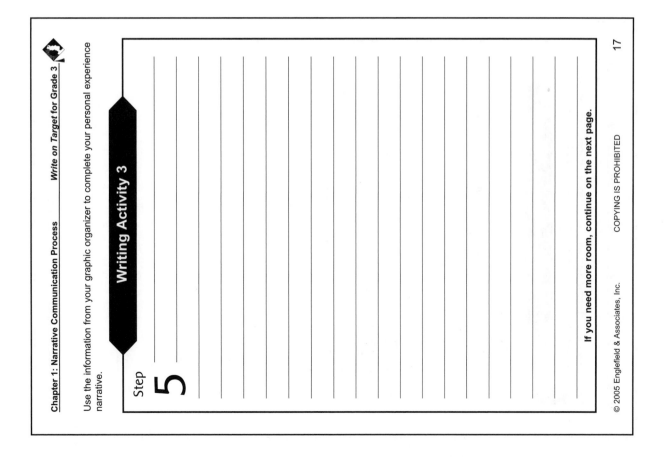

Use the information from your graphic organizer to complete your personal experience narrative.

Writing Activity 3

Step 5

If you need more room, continue on the next page.

17

Notes on Student Responses

Step 6

The checklist shows what your best personal experience narrative must include. Use the checklist below to review your work.

Checklist for Writing Activity 3

- ☐ My story has a title.

- ☐ My story is about a time I had to do something I didn't want to do, but it turned out to be a good experience.

- ☐ My story tells about the thing I didn't want to do.

- ☐ My story gives details about what made it turn into a good experience.

- ☐ My story has a beginning, middle, and end.

- ☐ I try to spell words correctly without using any help.

- ☐ I use interesting words.

- ☐ My sentences end with a period, an exclamation point, or a question mark.

- ☐ My sentences and proper names begin with a capital letter.

- ☐ I have written my story so that my reader can read my print or cursive writing.

Student Writing Activity 4: Personal Experience Narrative

Step 1   Follow along as the personal experience narrative "Camping Can Be Fun (or Maybe Not)" is read aloud.

Camping Can Be Fun (or Maybe Not)

I had always heard that camping out under the stars was a great experience. As my family drove to Lake Winneoba campground, I did not know about the adventure that I was going to have on my first camping trip.

Early that morning, I loaded the car with my important gear, which included a small tent, a sleeping bag, a bag of marshmallows, some chocolate bars, and a big bottle of bug spray. The sun glistened on the peaceful lake as we prepared the campsite. I thought that this night was going to be one of the best nights of my life. I put up my small tent, unrolled my sleeping bag, and prepared to roast my marshmallows over an open fire.

Smack! A small mosquito buzzed around my ears, and I sprayed the little beast. A small red bite began to itch. My father lit the fire and I put my fluffy marshmallow on a stick and shoved it into the flames. Unfortunately, my stick caught on fire and my marshmallow turned black. I burned my tongue as I put the whole thing in my mouth. Buzz! Another mosquito attacked my arm. I looked down and counted five itchy, red bites.

I climbed into my sleeping bag and prepared to listen to the sounds of the lake. Just as I was ready to fall asleep, I heard a clap of thunder and saw a flash of lightning. It started to rain. I could hear the rain lightly tapping on my canvas tent. Soon the rain began to pour, and a few raindrops fell on my head. It seemed like it was raining inside the tent! The rain soaked through my supposedly waterproof sleeping bag, and I could feel my wet pajamas cling to my legs. I think I fell asleep for only a few minutes during that entire night.

Early in the morning, I looked down at my arm and counted eleven mosquito bites. I tried to dry myself with a wet towel, rolled up my sleeping bag into a fat ball, ate an uncooked marshmallow, and went to sit in the car. I realized that during my first camping trip, I had not seen even one star—maybe next time.

Read the passage aloud. Students should follow along in their books. Then, students should complete the graphic organizer and the writing activity using the prompt on Student Workbook page 21.

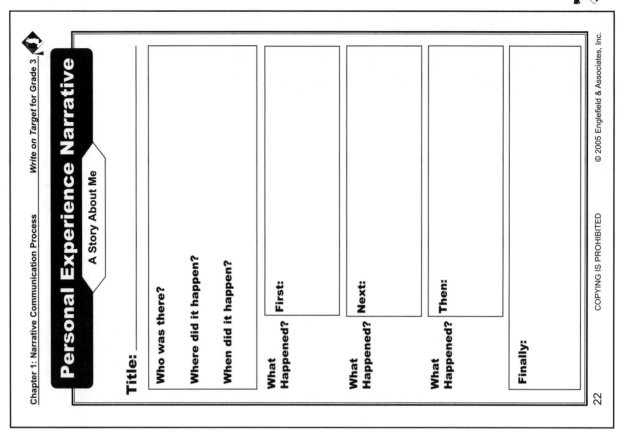

Personal Experience Narrative
A Story About Me

Title: _____

Who was there?

Where did it happen?

When did it happen?

What Happened?   **First:**

What Happened?   **Next:**

What Happened?   **Then:**

Finally:

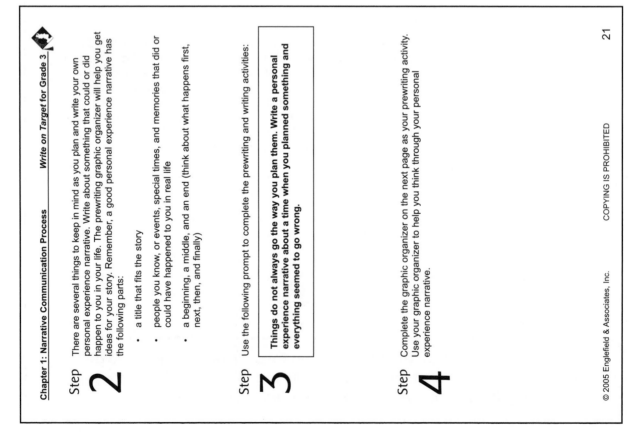

Step 2

There are several things to keep in mind as you plan and write your own personal experience narrative. Write about something that could or did happen to you in your life. The prewriting graphic organizer will help you get ideas for your story. Remember, a good personal experience narrative has the following parts:

- a title that fits the story

- people you know, or events, special times, and memories that did or could have happened to you in real life

- a beginning, a middle, and an end (think about what happens first, next, then, and finally)

Step 3

Use the following prompt to complete the prewriting and writing activities:

> **Things do not always go the way you plan them. Write a personal experience narrative about a time when you planned something and everything seemed to go wrong.**

Step 4

Complete the graphic organizer on the next page as your prewriting activity. Use your graphic organizer to help you think through your personal experience narrative.

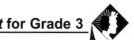
Writing Activity 4

Step 5

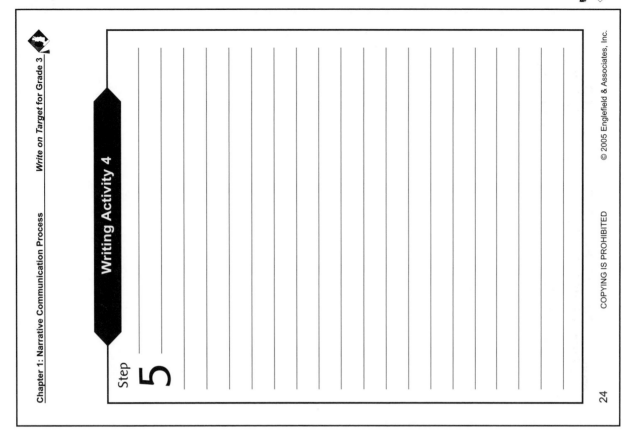

24

23

Use the information from your graphic organizer to complete your personal experience narrative.

Writing Activity 4

Step 5

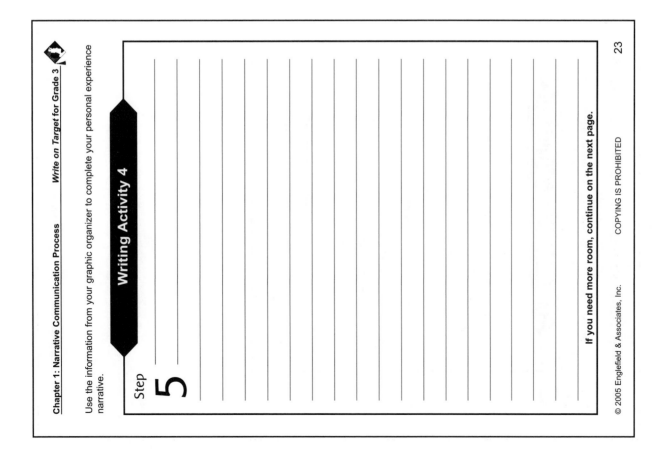

If you need more room, continue on the next page.

Notes on Student Responses

Step

6

The checklist shows what your best personal experience narrative must include. Use the checklist below to review your work.

Checklist for Writing Activity 4

☐ My story has a title.

☐ My story is about an experience that has happened to me or could happen to me.

☐ My story includes details about what I had planned.

☐ My story tells about the things that went wrong.

☐ My story has a beginning, middle, and end.

☐ I try to spell words correctly without using any help.

☐ I use interesting words.

☐ My sentences end with a period, an exclamation point, or a question mark.

☐ My sentences and proper names begin with a capital letter.

☐ I have written my story so that my reader can read my print or cursive writing.

Student Writing Activity 5: Retelling

Step **1**   Follow along as two passages are read. The first passage is a narrative titled "The Statue of Liberty: The Lady with the Iron Torch." The second passage is a retelling of "The Statue of Liberty: The Lady with the Iron Torch."

The Statue of Liberty: The Lady with the Iron Torch

My grandmother came to the United States from Poland over sixty years ago. She told me the story about how she arrived at Ellis Island near New York City with many other people from around the world. She had only sixteen dollars that she kept safely in her shoe. She saw the Statue of Liberty as she entered the United States and described the beautiful sight. She said that she would never forget her first view of the beautiful lady.

This summer I visited Ellis Island and saw the Statue of Liberty for the first time. As I stepped near her, I could not believe how large she was in real life. The torch was held high as the statue seemed to smile at all the people who entered the harbor. The statue's beautiful face had to be a wonderful sight for those who traveled great distances to enter America.

At the Immigration Museum on Ellis Island, I looked at the musical instruments, native costumes, and trunks of books that were brought to this country. I imagined what it was like to be a person entering the United States with sixteen dollars and a dream to be an American. My grandmother had great courage and determination just like the Statue of Liberty, the lady with the iron torch.

Read the passage and the retelling aloud. Students should follow along in their books. Then, students should complete the graphic organizer and the writing activity using the prompt on Student Workbook page 28.

        33

Step
1

Retelling of "The Statue of Liberty: The Lady with the Iron Torch"

Over sixty years ago the author's grandmother entered the United States from Poland. After a long voyage, she arrived at Ellis Island with people from many other countries. She only had sixteen dollars and a dream to be an American.

This summer the author was able to visit both Ellis Island and the Statue of Liberty. The Statue of Liberty looked large and beautiful as she greeted those who entered the harbor. Those entering through Ellis Island brought instruments, native clothing, and books. The author's grandmother had courage and a dream to become an American.

Read the retelling aloud. Students should follow along in their books. Then, students should complete the graphic organizer and the writing activity using the prompt on Student Workbook page 28.

34

Step 3

The Sloth and the Ants

When I was in third grade, I wrote a report on the two-toed sloth. That animal fascinated me. I could not believe that any creature could be so lazy that blue-green algae actually grew on it. Because they live upside down for at least 15 hours each day, their organs are in different positions from other mammals. Even their hair grows in the opposite direction. They move very slowly so they eat very little food. They do not even drink water because they eat juicy leaves.

I imagined a sloth hanging from every tree in the rainforest. I begged my parents to take me to a rainforest so that I could see the sloth not move. My parents finally took me to a rainforest in South America. I looked everywhere for the unusual animal. After the long trip, the only real rainforest creatures that I saw were cutter ants carrying large leaves across the ground. Somewhere in the canopy of the rainforest, the two-toed sloth rests and hides from visitors like me.

Step 2

There are several things to keep in mind as you plan and write your own retelling. In your retelling, you will write the story in your own words. The prewriting graphic organizer will help you organize your retelling. Remember, a good retelling has the following parts:

- the title of the story
- your own words to retell the story without adding any additional information
- what happened in the story, in the same order as it happened
- when and where the story takes place
- names of the characters in the story
- the beginning, middle, and end of the story

Step 3

Use the following prompt to complete the prewriting and writing activities:

> **Read the narrative titled "The Sloth and the Ants" on page 29. Retell the story so that the reader will know all the important facts of the story.**

Step 4

Complete the graphic organizer on page 30 as your prewriting activity. Use your graphic organizer to help you think through your retelling.

Use the information from your graphic organizer to complete your retelling.

Writing Activity 5

Step 5

If you need more room, continue on the next page.

Retelling
A Story I Retell in My Own Words

Notes from the Story

Title of the Story:

Who are the characters in the story?

Where does the story take place?

When does the story take place?

What is the purpose of the story?

Retell the Story in Order

How does the story begin?

What Happens?

First:

Next:

Then:

Finally:

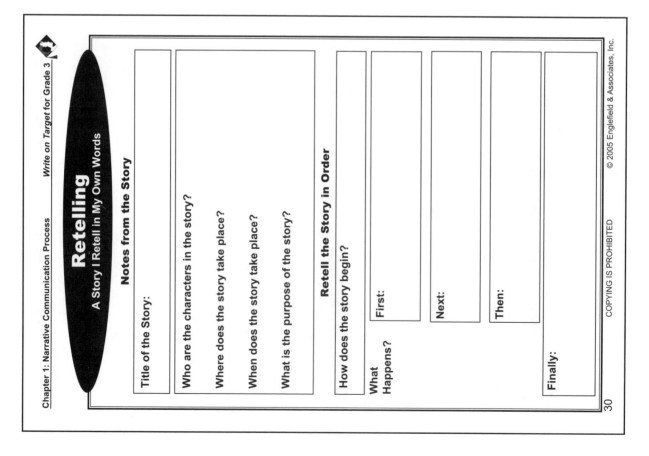

Step 6

The checklist shows what your best retelling must include. Use the checklist below to review your work.

Checklist for Writing Activity 5

☐ My retelling starts with the beginning of the story.

☐ My retelling tells the story in the same order.

☐ My retelling includes characters from the story.

☐ I use my own words to retell the story.

☐ My retelling includes a beginning, middle, and end.

☐ I use the details from the story. I do not add new details.

☐ I try to spell words correctly without using any help.

☐ My sentences and proper names begin with a capital letter.

☐ My sentences end with a period, an exclamation point, or a question mark.

☐ I have written my retelling so the reader can read my print or cursive writing.

33

Writing Activity 5

Step 5

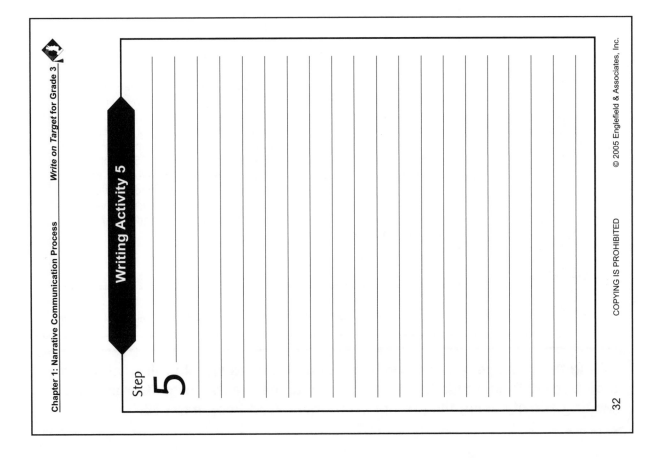

32

Student Writing Activity 6: Retelling

Step **1**   Follow along as two passages are read. The first passage is a narrative titled "The Animal Lover." The second passage is a retelling of "The Animal Lover."

The Animal Lover

I was spending the day with my Aunt Lila while my mom was working. We had been running errands, and we were going back to her house. We were almost home when we saw a small black and white dog in one of the yards. My aunt pointed at the dog and said, "Oh! Look at that poor little dog! He looks lost."

The dog seemed to be wandering around, and it didn't appear to be wearing a collar. We sat in the car for a few minutes while my aunt tried to decide what she should do. My aunt is very sweet, and she is a real animal lover. After a lot of thinking, she finally decided to take action—she went to get the dog.

The dog acted frightened when my aunt tried to get it into the car. The dog's reaction made my aunt even more certain the poor dog was lost. Once the dog was in the car, we were on our way to the veterinarian's office. We hoped the veterinarian might be able to help us track down the dog's owner. My aunt entered the veterinarian's office holding the misplaced dog in her arms. As soon as we walked in, the nurse said, "What's wrong with Pepper today?"

"Do you know this dog?" my aunt asked the nurse.

"Oh yes," said the nurse. "He lives on Valley Drive." When my aunt heard that, the expression on her face changed. Valley Drive was my aunt's home address! We quickly got back in the car with the dog. As we were heading back to Valley Drive, I saw something shiny near the dog's neck. I looked closer. Mostly hidden beneath the long fur was a collar and a tag that read, "My name is Pepper. I live at 8567 Valley Drive." I showed my aunt. She turned to me with wide eyes and said, "Oh my goodness—I just took this dog out of his own yard! I have to put him back right away!" We laughed as we drove to Valley Drive and put Pepper back in his yard. From then on, I always joked with my aunt about being a dognapper.

Read the passage and the retelling aloud. Students should follow along in their books. Then, students should complete the graphic organizer and the writing activity using the prompt on Student Workbook page 36.

Step

1

Retelling of "The Animal Lover"

The author and her aunt were on their way to the aunt's home. They saw a dog that they thought was lost, so they picked up the dog, put it in the car with them, and drove the dog to the veterinarian.

When they arrived at the veterinarian's office, a nurse recognized the dog right away. The nurse told the two where the dog lived. The dog lived on the same street as the aunt.

The author and her aunt left the veterinarian's office and took the dog back to where they had found it. On their way, the author found a tag on the dog's neck with the dog's name and address. The dog was named Pepper, and the aunt realized that she had taken Pepper from its owner's yard! From that point on, the author liked to tease her aunt and call her a "dognapper" because she had kidnapped the dog.

Read the retelling aloud. Students should follow along in their books. Then, students should complete the graphic organizer and the writing activity using the prompt on Student Workbook page 36.

Step 3

Bruce and Anthony

Bruce had only lived in New York for three weeks. He was just beginning to get used to his new apartment and new school. School was different at first because he didn't know anyone. Eventually, he met a few boys. Anthony was one of those boys. Anthony invited Bruce to come to his apartment to have dinner with his family. Bruce decided to go.

The next day after school, Bruce walked home with Anthony. The boys arrived at Anthony's apartment. They sat at the table and started their homework. As they sat there, Anthony's family members came home one by one. First, Anthony's mother arrived, then his father, and finally his older brother.

Bruce and Anthony gathered their books and went to play a game while Anthony's parents prepared dinner. When it was time for dinner, everyone sat at the table together. Bruce didn't say much; he just watched and listened. Anthony's family was so different from Bruce's family. Anthony's family talked and talked. They talked loudly and moved their hands quickly as they talked. At first, Bruce thought they might be arguing. He felt afraid. He looked at Anthony, but Anthony didn't seem to be upset, so Bruce continued to watch. Anthony's family members' faces looked happy. They smiled and laughed. Bruce wasn't afraid anymore.

Anthony's family ate different things than Bruce's family, too. One of the dishes they served was eggplant. Bruce had never had eggplant before, but he tried it. He liked it. After dinner, Bruce thanked Anthony's family for dinner and went home.

At home, Bruce talked with his mother about his dinner at Anthony's. He talked to her about how Anthony's family was not exactly like their family. As Bruce and his mother talked, Bruce realized how nice it is that families are different. He decided that life is interesting because of these differences. Bruce decided he would invite Anthony to his apartment for dinner sometime. Then, Anthony could see how Bruce's family was interesting, too.

Step 2

There are several things to keep in mind as you plan and write your own retelling. In your retelling, you will write the story in your own words. The prewriting graphic organizer will help you organize your retelling. Remember, a good retelling has the following parts:

- the title of the story
- your own words to retell the story without adding any additional information
- what happened in the story, in the same order as it happened
- when and where the story takes place
- names of the characters in the story
- the beginning, middle, and end of the story

Step 3

Use the following prompt to complete the prewriting and writing activities:

> **Read the narrative titled "Bruce and Anthony" on page 37. Retell the story so that the reader will know all the important facts of the story.**

Step 4

Complete the graphic organizer on page 38 as your prewriting activity. Use your graphic organizer to help you think through your retelling.

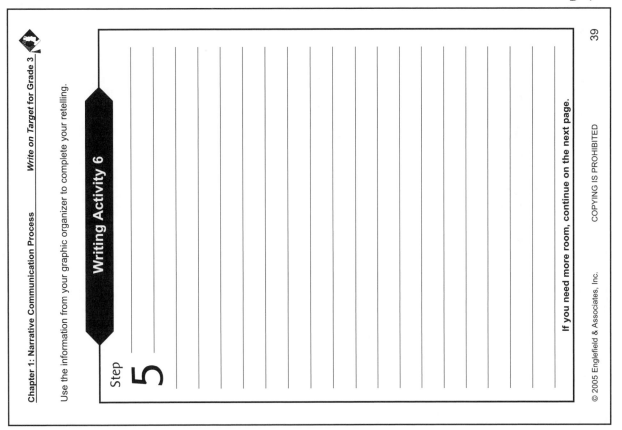

Writing Activity 6

Use the information from your graphic organizer to complete your retelling.

Step 5

_____
_____
_____
_____
_____
_____
_____
_____
_____
_____
_____

If you need more room, continue on the next page.

39

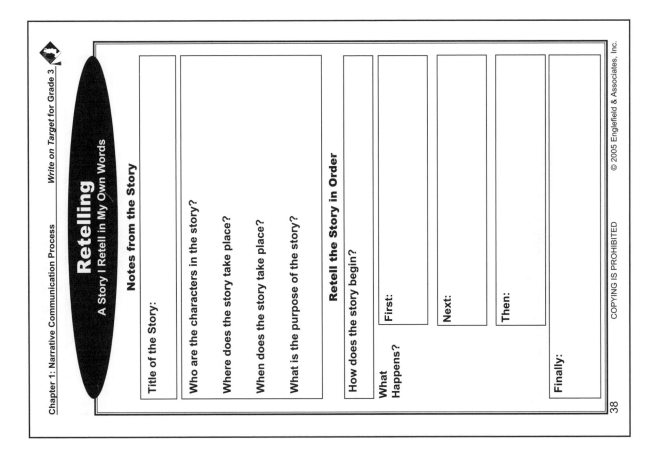

Retelling
A Story I Retell in My Own Words

Notes from the Story

Title of the Story:

Who are the characters in the story?

Where does the story take place?

When does the story take place?

What is the purpose of the story?

Retell the Story in Order

How does the story begin?

What Happens?

First:

Next:

Then:

Finally:

38

Step

6

The checklist shows what your best retelling must include. Use the checklist below to review your work.

Checklist for Writing Activity 6

☐ My retelling starts with the beginning of the story.

☐ My retelling tells the story in the same order.

☐ My retelling includes characters from the story.

☐ I use my own words to retell the story.

☐ My retelling includes a beginning, middle, and end.

☐ I use the details from the story. I do not add new details.

☐ I try to spell words correctly without using any help.

☐ My sentences and proper names begin with a capital letter.

☐ My sentences end with a period, an exclamation point, or a question mark.

☐ I have written my retelling so the reader can read my print or cursive writing.

Writing Activity 6

Step

5

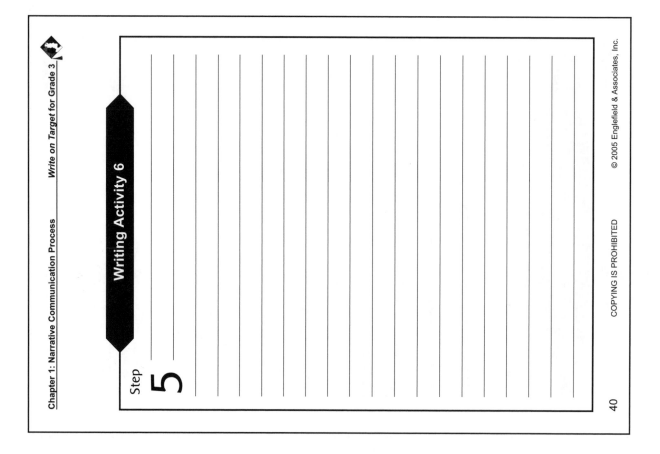

Additional Writing Prompts for a Fictional Narrative:

1. Write a fairy tale about a character who has an adventure.

2. Write a narrative in which the character or characters learn a valuable lesson such as being kind to someone.

3. Write a fictional narrative about an American hero whom you created. Make certain that the character has characteristics that you admire.

4. After hearing the stories of people who have survived hardships, write a story to share with your class about a brave character.

5. Think of a place that interests you. Write a story to share with a friend about that place. Include interesting characters.

6. Write a story about something that happened on your character's birthday or any other memorable day in your character's life.

Additional Writing Prompts for a Personal Experience Narrative:

1. Write a personal experience narrative about a time when you were brave. Write it so that the reader can feel why you were so courageous.

2. Write a personal experience narrative entitled: "The Best Day Ever."

3. Tell a story about a memorable event in your life.

4. Write a personal experience narrative about a time you spent with your favorite animal at home, at the zoo, or in your imagination.

5. Share a story about a favorite memory. Help your reader experience the unforgettable events of this memory.

6. Tell the story about a time when a person made you smile (or even laugh out loud).

Additional Writing Prompts for a Retelling:

1. After watching a movie or documentary on a historical event, retell the story in your own words.

2. Retell a story from a book, newspaper, or magazine.

3. Retell a family story that you have often heard at a gathering of family or friends.

4. Retell a recent news story that you heard on the radio or on television.

5. Retell your favorite poem, story, fairy tale, or fable.

2 The Descriptive Communication Process

(Journal and Descriptive Letter)

The purposes of this chapter include:

1 Showing how the descriptive communication process links to the writing modes.

2 Discussing the purpose and features of a descriptive letter and a journal.

3 Offering teaching tips on where students break down in the descriptive process.

4 Providing ideas for the development of additional writing prompts for journals and letters.

> The following teaching tools will be provided for a **journal** and a **descriptive letter**: graphic organizers, two writing prompts, and student checklists.

What is the Descriptive Communication Process?

The purpose of description is to provide a sensory picture of a person, place, or thing with vivid written details. Two examples of the descriptive communication process are the journal and the descriptive letter. Journals have been used and defined in a variety of ways—writer's notebooks, dialogue journals, personal journals or diaries, learning logs, and project journals. A journal can be written in paragraph or letter form. Some ideas to help students generate thoughts for a journal include: memories, hobbies, current events, questions, pets, plans, hopes, discoveries, and personal news.

Letters must be written in the proper form: a date, a greeting, a body, a closing, and a signature are included. The topic will serve as the motivation for writing. Each letter will have a specific audience to address; however, an important thing to keep in mind is that the audience often varies from one letter to another.

Descriptions contain vivid sensory experiences and many specific details. The reader can imagine the person, place, or thing the writer describes. The written piece tells how the writer perceives the subject matter through as many senses as possible—sights, sounds, tastes, tactile sensations, and movement. A single person, place, or thing is often the major focal point for each descriptive section.

Features of a Journal

- Often the audience is oneself.

- The purpose is to record thoughts, feelings, and personal events.

- The format is often in paragraph form.

- The personal journal is often written in an informal style of writing.

Features of a Letter

- The audience is specific, and the purpose is often a personal communication.

- Clearly addresses the audience with the intent to communicate

- Contains a greeting, a body, and a closing

- Written with a very specific purpose

Correlation of Descriptive Communication to the Writing Modes

Below are the writing modes that reflect the importance of the descriptive communication process. The ability to describe is embedded in virtually all writing tasks and formats. Good writers describe so readers can experience what the authors want their audiences to experience. The journal and the descriptive letter were selected as the formats for students to practice and refine their descriptive skills.

Journal – a piece of writing that includes a date and a description of the writer's feelings, or the sights, sounds, events, and people the writer has encountered. Often, the audience is the writer.

Descriptive Letter – a piece of writing that has a specific form which includes a date, a greeting, a body, a closing, and a signature. A letter addresses a specific audience and establishes a written connection with that audience.

Teaching Tips: Where Students Break Down in the Descriptive Communication Process

- Students do not use sufficient details to recreate the picture.

- Students use unnecessary details to recreate the picture.

- Students have a tendency to shift into other modes, especially narrative.

- Students want to tell the reader what to think about the person, place, thing, or event, rather than showing the reader through vivid descriptions so the reader can form his or her own mental pictures. For example, a student may write, "*The girl was angry,*" rather than, "*The girl raised her clenched fist, and her face was bright red.*"

- In letter formats, students often do not establish a personal connection with the reader. Students omit either opening or closing comments. Examples of acceptable comments are listed below.

Sample opening comments:

Hope all is well with you…

I hope this letter finds you well…

I enjoyed our last visit …

I enjoyed your last letter …

Sample closing comments:

I look forward to seeing you…

Hope to see you soon…

Please write and tell me more about…

Student Writing Activity 7: A Descriptive Journal

Step
1
Follow along as the May 4, 2006 journal entry is read aloud.

May 4, 2006
Journal Entry

Today started out to be just another day. The alarm went off, and my mother stuck her head in my room to say good morning and to make sure I was up and moving. I slowly got dressed, only opening my eyes enough to make sure everything matched. Breakfast was my usual bowl of cereal with sliced bananas, which I slurped up in time to catch the bus. I went to school and made it through the day. When I came out of school, the sun was shining and the weather was getting warmer. Finally, I was on the bus and on my way home.

There I was, sitting on the stuffy, bumpy bus packed three-to-a-seat with 40 other kids. Some of them were doing homework, some were screaming, some were sleeping, and occasionally, a wad of paper would fly by my head. I was looking out the window and what I saw made me sit straight up.

There it was. The sign read OPEN FOR THE SEASON. I leaned back in my seat and I closed my eyes. I could picture myself sitting outside at the table under the umbrella eating my swirlie. I could almost taste it ,so cold and creamy with chunks of tasty peanut butter. Tonight after dinner, I ate my first swirlie of the season. It was everything I had hoped. That swirlie was the first of the season, but it won't be the last!

Read the journal entry aloud. Students should follow along in their books. Then, students should complete the graphic organizer and the writing activity using the prompt on Student Workbook page 45.

Journal Entry

What day will you write about in your journal entry?

Why are you writing about this day?

Who was there?

Where did it happen?

When did it happen?

What Happened? First:

What Happened? Next:

What Happened? Then:

Finally:

How did it make you and others feel?

46   COPYING IS PROHIBITED   © 2005 Englefield & Associates, Inc.

Step 2

There are several things to keep in mind as you plan and write your journal entry. Remember, a good journal entry has the following parts:

- a date
- a description of the sights and sounds of the events or people
- a description of your feelings
- a beginning, a middle, and an end

Step 3

Use the following prompt to complete the prewriting and writing activities:

> Write a journal entry about a simple thing that makes you happy. It could be a smile or a hug, a phone call or a visit with someone special, eating at a favorite restaurant, a special place, or maybe a daydream. Be sure to describe that simple thing and the way it makes you feel.

Step 4

Complete the graphic organizer on the next page as your prewriting activity. Use your graphic organizer to help you think through your journal entry.

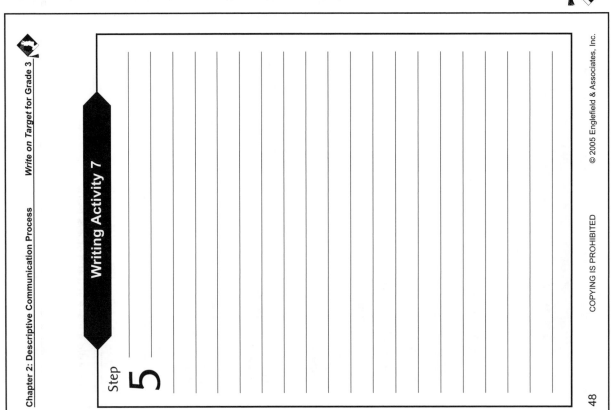

Chapter 2: Descriptive Communication Process — *Write on Target* for Grade 3

COPYING IS PROHIBITED

Writing Activity 7

Step **5**

48

© 2005 Englefield & Associates, Inc.

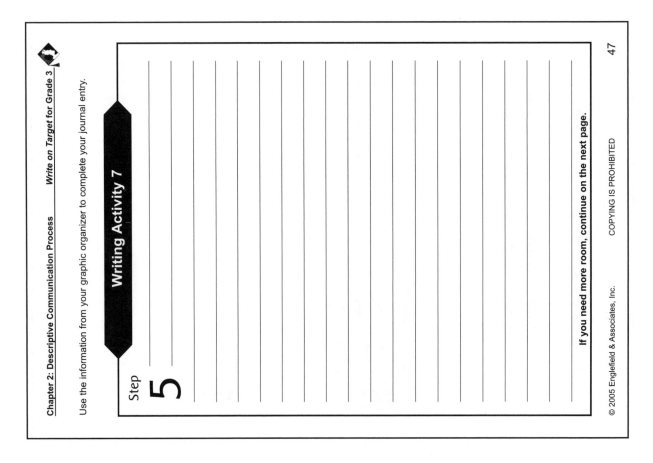

Chapter 2: Descriptive Communication Process — *Write on Target* for Grade 3

Use the information from your graphic organizer to complete your journal entry.

Writing Activity 7

Step **5**

If you need more room, continue on the next page.

© 2005 Englefield & Associates, Inc.

COPYING IS PROHIBITED

47

Notes on Student Responses

Step 6

The checklist shows what your best journal entry must include. Use the checklist below to review your work.

Checklist for Writing Activity 7

- ☐ My journal entry has a date.
- ☐ I describe the people, places, things, or events that make me happy with all or some of the following words: looks like, sounds like, does, thinks, makes other people feel, or makes me feel.
- ☐ My journal entry has a beginning, middle, and end.
- ☐ I try to spell words correctly without using any help.
- ☐ I use interesting words.
- ☐ My sentences and proper names begin with a capital letter.
- ☐ My sentences end with a period, an exclamation point, or a question mark.
- ☐ I have written my journal entry so the reader can read my print or cursive writing.

49

Student Writing Activity 8: A Descriptive Journal

Write on Target **for Grade 3**

Step **1**   Follow along as the October 28, 2007 journal entry is read aloud.

October 28, 2007
Journal Entry

Today I finished my first chapter book. It was called <u>Charlotte's Web</u>, and it was written by E.B. White. I read many of the pages by myself, and my teacher, Mrs. Strosoff, also read some of the chapters to us. I am happy that I read the book and always want to remember why it was important to me.

My favorite character is Wilbur, the pig. He has some wonderful times with a girl called Fern. Fern learns that Wilbur is being fattened because her family is planning to sell him for food. An amazing thing happens with a spider named Charlotte. She spins messages in her web so that everyone will think that her friend Wilbur is special—messages like "SOME PIG." Wilbur is taken to the fair and wins a ribbon for best pig.

I will always remember how happy and relieved I felt when Charlotte saved Wilbur's life. I hope to read other chapter books, but I will always remember the story of Wilbur the wonderful pig and his spider friend.

Read the journal entry aloud. Students should follow along in their books. Then, students should complete the graphic organizer and the writing activity using the prompt on Student Workbook page 51.

52

Journal Entry

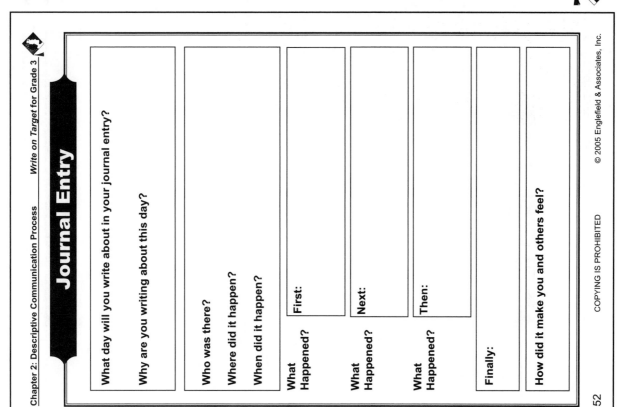

What day will you write about in your journal entry?

Why are you writing about this day?

Who was there?

Where did it happen?

When did it happen?

What Happened?   First:

What Happened?   Next:

What Happened?   Then:

Finally:

How did it make you and others feel?

Step 2

There are several things to keep in mind as you plan and write your journal entry. Remember, a good journal entry has the following parts:

- a date
- a description of the sights and sounds of the events or people
- a description of your feelings
- a beginning, a middle, and an end

Step 3

Use the following prompt to complete the prewriting and writing activities:

> Write a journal entry that describes something that you have read or seen that you will always remember. Be sure to tell how the memory makes you feel.

Step 4

Complete the graphic organizer on the next page as your prewriting activity. Use your graphic organizer to help you think through your journal entry.

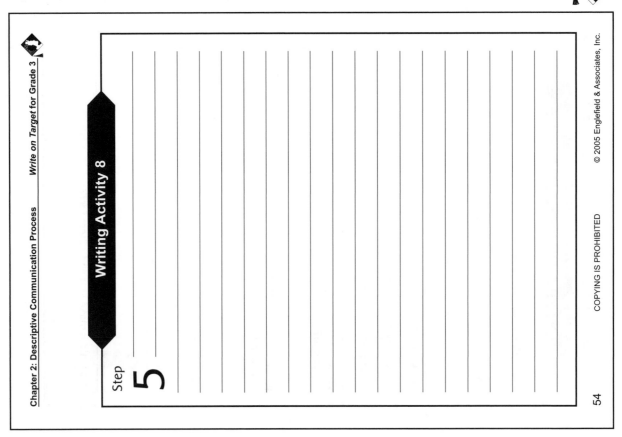

Writing Activity 8

Step 5

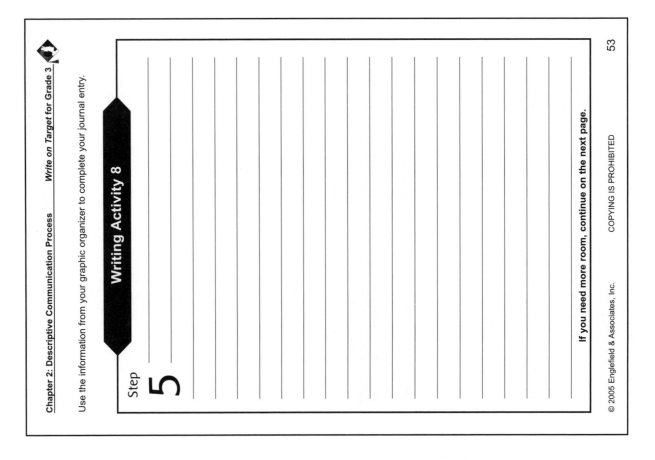

Use the information from your graphic organizer to complete your journal entry.

Writing Activity 8

Step 5

If you need more room, continue on the next page.

Notes on Student Responses

Step

6

The checklist shows what your best journal entry must include. Use the checklist below to review your work.

▶ Checklist for Writing Activity 8

☐ My journal entry has a date.

☐ I describe the memorable thing that I read or saw using all or some of the following words: looks like, sounds like, does, thinks, makes other people feel, or makes me feel.

☐ My journal entry has a beginning, middle, and end.

☐ I try to spell words correctly without using any help.

☐ I use interesting words.

☐ My sentences and proper names begin with a capital letter.

☐ My sentences end with a period, an exclamation point, or a question mark.

☐ I have written my journal entry so the reader can read my print or cursive writing.

Student Writing Activity 9: A Descriptive Letter

Step

1

Follow along as the descriptive letter is read aloud.

— *Courtney* —

February 9, 2007

Dear Grandma,

As I went through the grocery store with my mom today, I asked if we could buy the ingredients to make cookies. It made me feel really happy as I saw the various ingredients go into our cart. After we got home, I tried to figure out why that experience made me feel that way.

When I think of making cookies, it brings back all those memories of the times we were rolling out the sticky dough and using the heart-shaped cookie cutters to make cookies for Valentine's Day. There was always white flour scattered all over the kitchen, but we never worried about it. We just kept baking our cookies of love, one batch after the other. As we baked, the entire house was filled with the warm, homey smell of sugar cookies.

I just had to write to you to tell you what I figured out. The more I thought about those cookies, the more I realized it wasn't the cookies that made me feel so happy, Grandma. It's you. It's the love you shared with me as we baked those cookies together that brings me the memories I will always be able to keep.

I love you,

Courtney

56   COPYING IS PROHIBITED   © 2005 Englefield & Associates, Inc.

Read the letter aloud. Students should follow along in their books. Then, students should complete the graphic organizer and the writing activity using the prompt on Student Workbook page 57.

Descriptive Letter

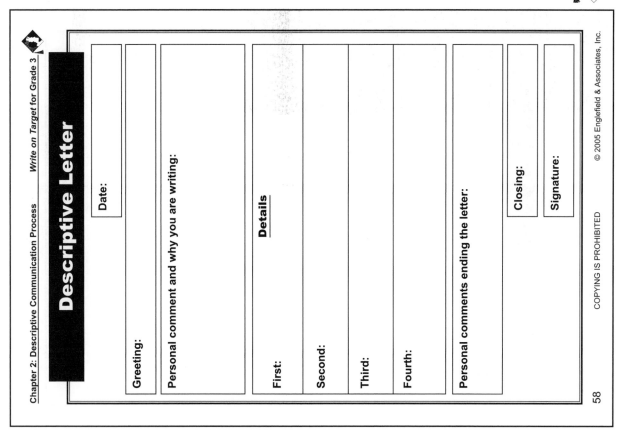

Date:

Greeting:

Personal comment and why you are writing:

Details

First:

Second:

Third:

Fourth:

Personal comments ending the letter:

Closing:

Signature:

Step 2

There are several things to keep in mind as you plan and write your descriptive letter. Remember, a good descriptive letter has the following parts:

- a date
- a greeting
- a body that talks to the reader
- a closing
- a signature

Step 3

Use the following prompt to complete the prewriting and writing activities:

> **Write a letter to someone about a special time you spent with him or her. Tell the person what you enjoy remembering about that time.**

Step 4

Complete the graphic organizer on the next page as your prewriting activity. Use your graphic organizer to help you think through your descriptive letter.

Use the information from your graphic organizer to complete your descriptive letter.

Writing Activity 9

Step 5

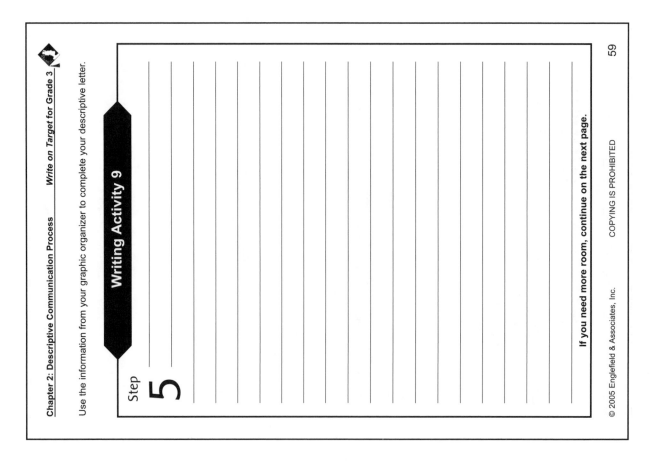

If you need more room, continue on the next page.

Writing Activity 9

Step 5

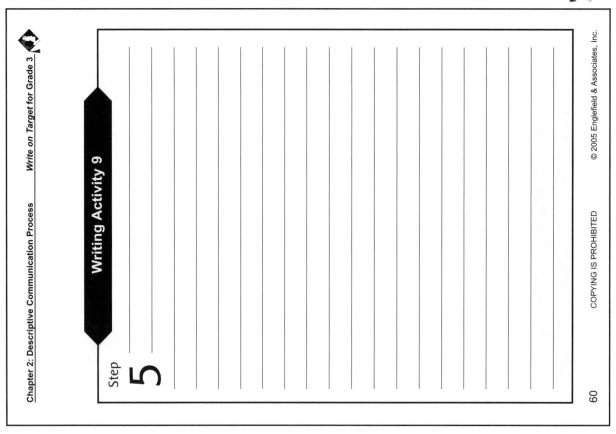

Notes on Student Responses

Step

6

The checklist shows what your best descriptive letter must include. Use the checklist below to review your work.

Checklist for Writing Activity 9

☐ I use the form for a letter with a date, greeting, body, closing, and signature.

☐ My letter tells my reader why I am writing and makes personal comments.

☐ My letter describes the special time I spent with the person: what we did, where we were, and what happened.

☐ My descriptive letter includes a personal closing comment.

☐ I try to spell words correctly without using any help.

☐ I use interesting words.

☐ My sentences and proper names begin with a capital letter.

☐ My sentences end with a period, an exclamation point, or a question mark.

☐ I have written my letter so the reader can read my print or cursive writing.

Student Writing Activity 10: A Descriptive Letter

Step

1

Follow along as the descriptive letter is read aloud.

A note from Alex

June 17, 2006

Dear Tooth Fairy,

I hope that this letter finds you well as you travel all over the world collecting teeth from boys and girls. I know that you are very busy. I am writing you to tell you about my missing tooth. If you look in my mouth, you will see that my tooth really is missing.

Today, I was playing with Chip, my golden retriever. Chip is a great dog, but as I was throwing a stick for him to catch, he bumped me in the mouth. My tooth was loose, and it fell somewhere in the grass in my yard. I looked and looked for the tooth, but I could not find it.

I made a tooth out of green clay to put under my pillow. My real tooth was white. I would like you to know that I did brush it every day. I hope you will understand as you put the green tooth in your tooth fairy bag.

I appreciate all you do for boys and girls like me. I will be more careful next time, since I have many more teeth to lose. I hope to see you someday.

Your friend,

Alex

Read the letter aloud. Students should follow along in their books. Then, students should complete the graphic organizer and the writing activity using the prompt on Student Workbook page 63.

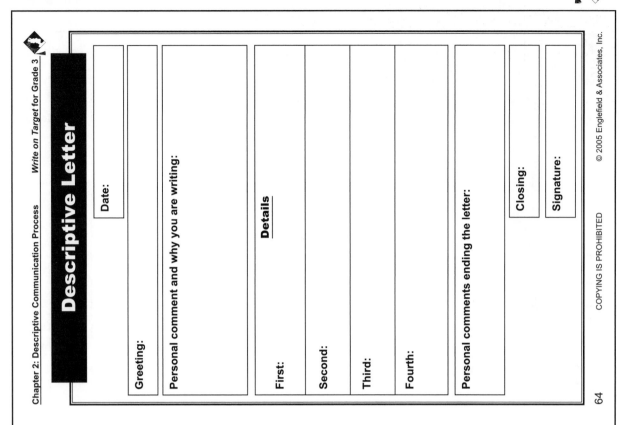

Descriptive Letter

Date:

Greeting:

Personal comment and why you are writing:

Details

First:

Second:

Third:

Fourth:

Personal comments ending the letter:

Closing:

Signature:

64   COPYING IS PROHIBITED   © 2005 Englefield & Associates, Inc.

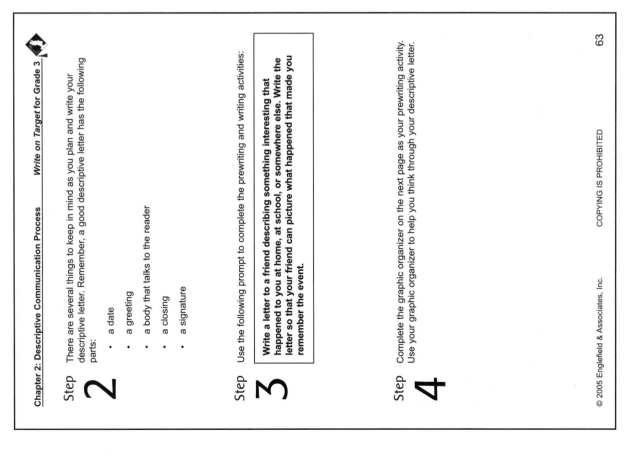

Step 2

There are several things to keep in mind as you plan and write your descriptive letter. Remember, a good descriptive letter has the following parts:

- a date
- a greeting
- a body that talks to the reader
- a closing
- a signature

Step 3

Use the following prompt to complete the prewriting and writing activities:

> **Write a letter to a friend describing something interesting that happened to you at home, at school, or somewhere else. Write the letter so that your friend can picture what happened that made you remember the event.**

Step 4

Complete the graphic organizer on the next page as your prewriting activity. Use your graphic organizer to help you think through your descriptive letter.

© 2005 Englefield & Associates, Inc.   COPYING IS PROHIBITED   63

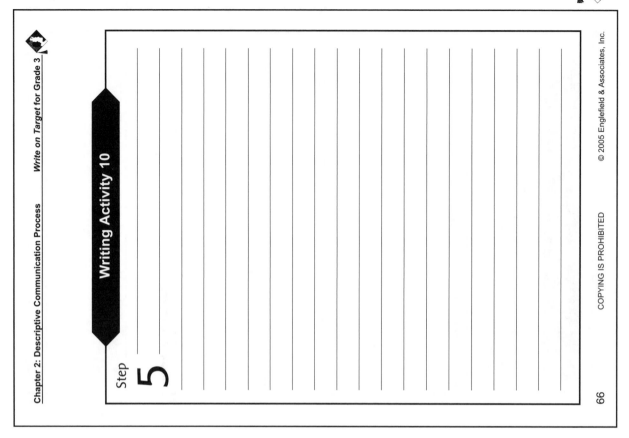

Writing Activity 10

Step 5

66

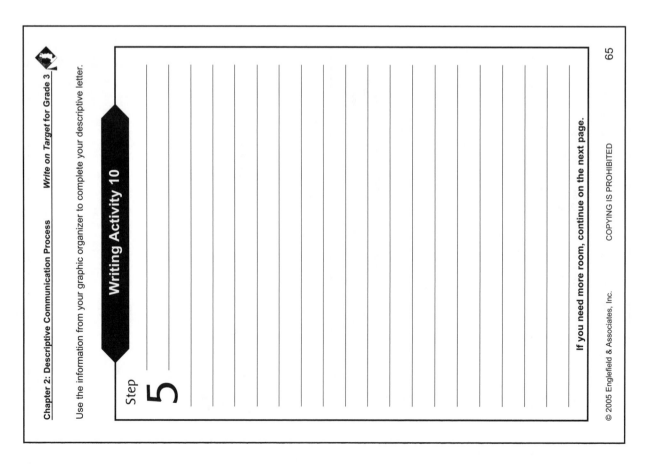

Use the information from your graphic organizer to complete your descriptive letter.

Writing Activity 10

Step 5

If you need more room, continue on the next page.

65

Notes on Student Responses

Step

6

The checklist shows what your best descriptive letter must include. Use the checklist below to review your work.

Checklist for Writing Activity 10

- ☐ I use the form for a letter with a date, greeting, body, closing, and signature.

- ☐ My letter tells my reader why I am writing and makes personal comments.

- ☐ My letter describes an interesting thing that happened to me.

- ☐ My descriptive letter includes a personal closing comment.

- ☐ I try to spell words correctly without using any help.

- ☐ I use interesting words.

- ☐ My sentences and proper names begin with a capital letter.

- ☐ My sentences end with a period, an exclamation point, or a question mark.

- ☐ I have written my letter so the reader can read my print or cursive writing.

Additional Writing Prompts for a Journal Entry:

1. Describe your favorite activity.

2. Describe a holiday, special occasion, or celebration that is part of a tradition with your class, family, or friends.

3. Describe a famous person whom you have heard or read about.

4. Describe what you like most about yourself.

5. Record in your journal a description of something or someone from your home or school you always want to remember.

Additional Writing Prompts for a Descriptive Letter:

1. Write a letter to the person in history you most admire. In your letter, describe why you think he or she is an important part of the past.

2. The radio station in your town is sponsoring a contest to provide a special trip for the kindest person they can find. Pick someone and write a letter to the station explaining why that person should win.

3. Write a letter to a friend about a place the two of you are going to see when your friend comes to visit you. Describe this place so your friend will feel excited about coming.

4. You ordered something from a catalog or from the internet. When the box arrived, you realized it was not what you wanted. Write a letter to the company describing why you are returning the item.

5. Write a letter to the principal nominating your teacher for "Teacher of the Year." Give reasons why your teacher deserves this award.

6. Write a letter to a person in another country describing what life is like in America.

3 The Direction Communication Process

(Directions and Invitation)

The purposes of this chapter include:

1   Showing how the direction communication process links to the writing modes.

2   Discussing the purpose and features of directions and an invitation.

3   Offering teaching tips on where students break down in the direction process.

4   Providing ideas for the development of additional writing prompts for directions and an invitation.

> The following teaching tools are provided for a **set of directions** and an **invitation**: graphic organizers, two writing prompts, and student checklists.

What is the Direction Communication Process?

The purpose of the direction communication process is to provide a set of actions that lead to a goal, such as going somewhere or making something. Two examples of the direction communication process are directions and an invitation.

Features of Directions

- Provides communication that is orderly and efficient

- Assumes the person that is being directed is not familiar with the task

- Is written in correct chronological order or consecutive order

Words that Provide Directions

- direction words: right, left, north, south, east, west

- prepositions: in, on, under, before, after

- adverbial phrases: when you see the…; before you reach the…; after you pass the…

- direction verbs: mix, blend, stir, insert, pour

Features of an Invitation

- An invitation tells who is invited and who is hosting the event.

- An invitation indicates the type of event.

- An invitation indicates the time and date of the event, as well as RSVP details.

- An invitation indicates where the event will take place and often includes a map to the location.

Correlation of Direction Communication to the Writing Modes

Directions – a piece of writing that explains how to do something or how to go somewhere. It clearly describes the materials that are needed to complete the task and uses step-by-step order. Directions may be written in paragraph form or line-by-line. A starting point and and ending point are included.

Invitation – a piece of writing that can be in letter format. An invitation includes the purpose of the invitation, who is writing the invitation, who is being invited, where and when the event takes place, and any other important information.

 ## Teaching Tips: Where Students Break Down in the Direction Communication Process

- Students leave out information important to the completion of the task or goal because they assume that the reader knows what the student knows.

- Students provide more information than is necessary for the efficient completion of the task—they distract the reader with too much information.

- Students do not understand or do not use "direction words."

- Students tend to switch into other communication modes, especially narrative.

                   © 2005 Englefield & Associates, Inc.

Student Writing Activity 11: Directions (How to Do Something)

Step 1   Follow along as the directions "Planting a Seed" are read aloud.

Planting a Seed

In the spring, it can be fun to plant some seeds and watch them grow into plants. You will need a container, seeds, rocks, and soil.

1. Get a container such as a cup, a deep bowl, or a flower pot.

2. Put enough rocks in the container to cover the bottom of the container. Fill the container with soil.

3. Use your finger or a spoon to dig a small hole about an inch deep and two inches wide in the middle of the soil.

4. Place a few seeds in the hole and cover the seeds with soil. After you cover the seeds with the soil, pat the soil gently.

5. Pour some water in the container over the soil and seeds.

Finally, be sure to place your container in the sun and water your seeds whenever the soil gets dry. If you do all of this, you will soon get to enjoy watching your seeds grow into a plant!

> **Read the directions aloud. Students should follow along in their books. Then, students should complete the graphic organizer and the writing activity using the prompt on Student Workbook page 71.**

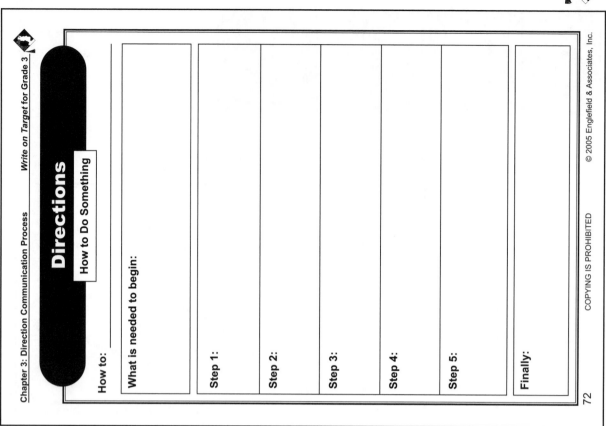

Directions

How to Do Something

How to:

What is needed to begin:

Step 1:

Step 2:

Step 3:

Step 4:

Step 5:

Finally:

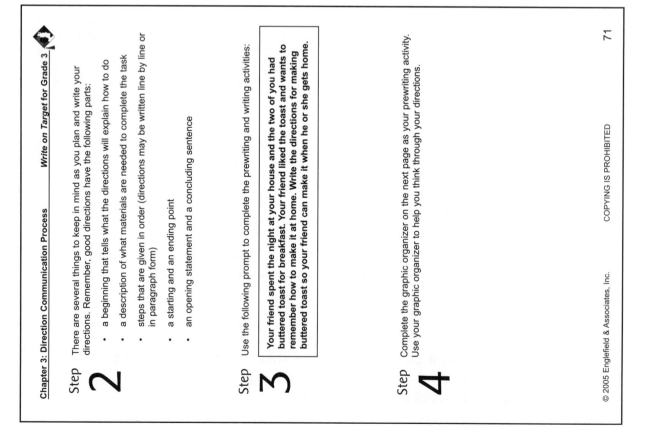

Step 2

There are several things to keep in mind as you plan and write your directions. Remember, good directions have the following parts:

- a beginning that tells what the directions will explain how to do
- a description of what materials are needed to complete the task
- steps that are given in order (directions may be written line by line or in paragraph form)
- a starting and an ending point
- an opening statement and a concluding sentence

Step 3

Use the following prompt to complete the prewriting and writing activities:

> **Your friend spent the night at your house and the two of you had buttered toast for breakfast. Your friend liked the toast and wants to remember how to make it at home. Write the directions for making buttered toast so your friend can make it when he or she gets home.**

Step 4

Complete the graphic organizer on the next page as your prewriting activity. Use your graphic organizer to help you think through your directions.

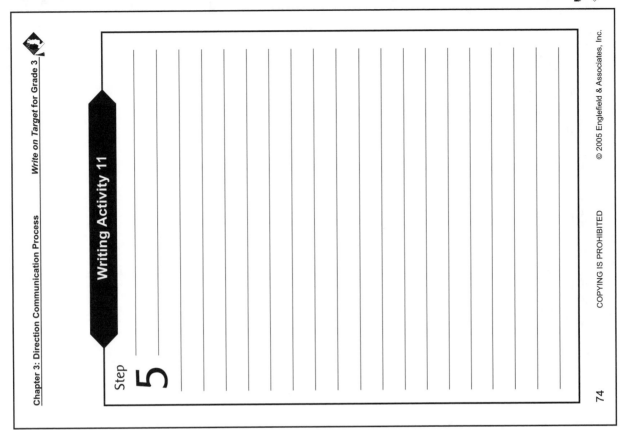

Writing Activity 11

Step

5

74

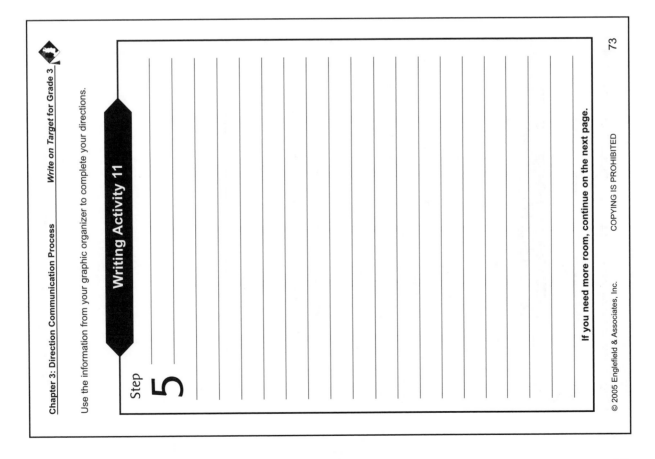

Use the information from your graphic organizer to complete your directions.

Writing Activity 11

Step

5

If you need more room, continue on the next page.

73

Notes on Student Responses

Step

6

The checklist shows what your best directions must include. Use the checklist below to review your work.

Checklist for Writing Activity 11

- ☐ My set of directions begins with a sentence telling what my directions will explain how to do.

- ☐ My set of directions clearly describes the materials that are needed to complete the task.

- ☐ My set of directions uses the correct order to tell my friend what to do first, next, and so on to make the toast.

- ☐ My set of directions has a concluding sentence describing the buttered toast.

- ☐ I try to spell words correctly without using any help.

- ☐ I use interesting words.

- ☐ My sentences and proper names begin with a capital letter.

- ☐ My sentences end with a period, an exclamation point, or a question mark.

- ☐ I have written my directions so the reader can read my print or cursive writing.

Student Writing Activity 12: Directions (How to Go Somewhere)

Write on Target for Grade 3

Step 1   Look at the map below. Follow along as the set of directions for finding the car rider pickup area are read aloud.

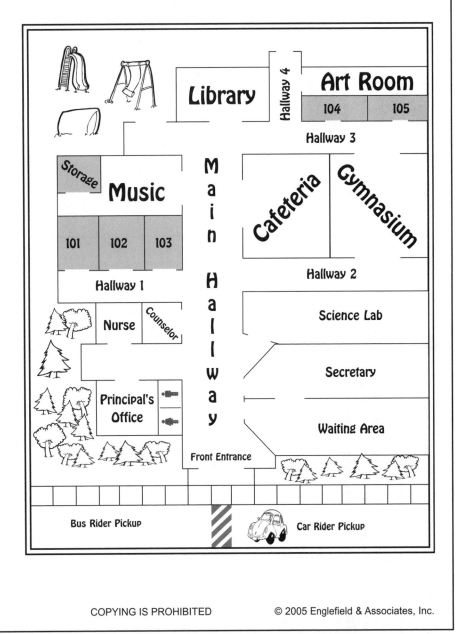

Read the passage aloud. Students should follow along in their books. Then, students should complete the graphic organizer and the writing activity using the prompt on Student Workbook page 78.

Step 2

There are several things to keep in mind as you plan and write your own directions. Remember, good directions have the following parts:

- a beginning that tells where the directions begin and end
- a description of what is needed to complete the task
- steps that are given in order
- a starting point and an ending point

Step 3

Use the following prompt to complete the prewriting and writing activities:

> **A new student has been placed in your classroom. Your teacher has asked you to help the student find her way around the school. The new student needs to get from the playground to the nurse's office each day to get medication. The new student can't remember how to get there. Use the map on page 79 to help you write directions for the new student so she can find the nurse's office each day.**

Step 4

Complete the graphic organizer on page 80 as your prewriting activity. Use your graphic organizer to help you think through your directions.

Step 1

> **Claude is a new student. He is a car rider. His last class of the day is in the art room. Write directions for him so he can get from the art room to the car rider pickup area.**
>
> To get from the art room to the car rider pickup area, follow these directions.
>
> 1. First, walk out of the art room and turn left into hallway 4.
> 2. Walk to the end of hallway 4, and turn right into hallway 3.
> 3. When you reach the library entrance, turn left into the main hallway.
> 4. Walk down the main hallway past the cafeteria, the science lab, and the waiting area.
> 5. Go outside through the front entrance of the school. Once you are outside, turn left and walk down the sidewalk.
>
> Keep walking and the car rider pickup area will be on the right. Find the right car, and you will be on your way home!

Directions

How to Go Somewhere

Where are you going? _____

Where to start:

First:

Second:

Third:

Fourth:

Fifth:

Where you finish:

Step 3

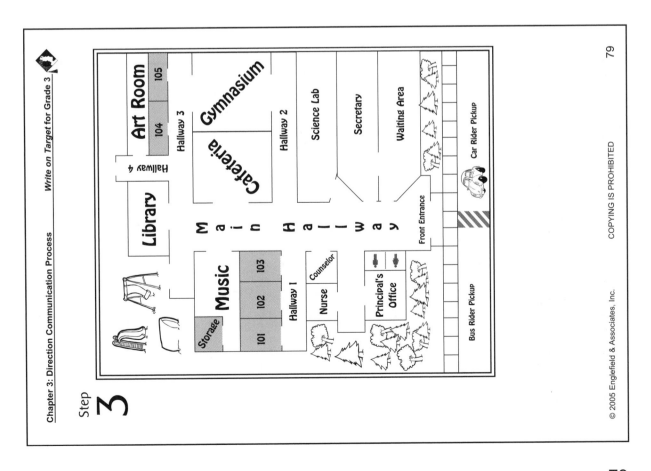

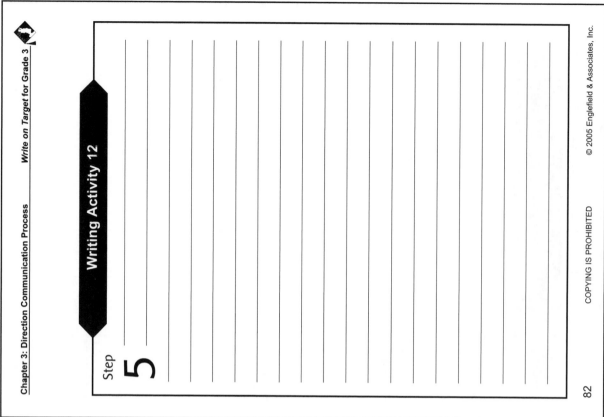

Writing Activity 12

Step 5

82

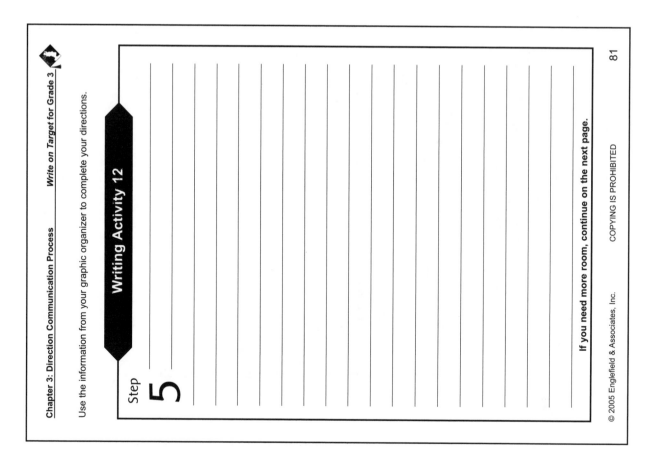

Use the information from your graphic organizer to complete your directions.

Writing Activity 12

Step 5

If you need more room, continue on the next page.

81

Notes on Student Responses

Step 6

The checklist shows what your best directions must include. Use the checklist below to review your work.

◆ Checklist for Writing Activity 12

☐ My set of directions begins with a sentence telling where my directions begin and end.

☐ My set of directions uses step-by-step order (1, 2, 3, 4, …) to tell my friend where to go first, next, and so on.

☐ My set of directions gives accurate details and directions for traveling.

☐ I try to spell words correctly without using any help.

☐ I use interesting words.

☐ My sentences and proper names begin with a capital letter.

☐ My sentences end with a period, an exclamation point, or a question mark.

☐ I have written my directions so the reader can read my print or cursive writing.

83

Student Writing Activity 13: An Invitation

Step **1**　Follow along as the invitation below is read aloud.

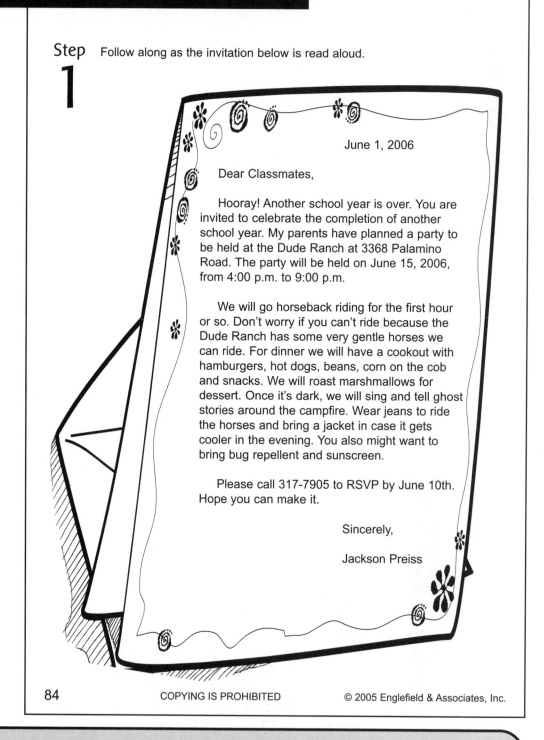

June 1, 2006

Dear Classmates,

Hooray! Another school year is over. You are invited to celebrate the completion of another school year. My parents have planned a party to be held at the Dude Ranch at 3368 Palamino Road. The party will be held on June 15, 2006, from 4:00 p.m. to 9:00 p.m.

We will go horseback riding for the first hour or so. Don't worry if you can't ride because the Dude Ranch has some very gentle horses we can ride. For dinner we will have a cookout with hamburgers, hot dogs, beans, corn on the cob and snacks. We will roast marshmallows for dessert. Once it's dark, we will sing and tell ghost stories around the campfire. Wear jeans to ride the horses and bring a jacket in case it gets cooler in the evening. You also might want to bring bug repellent and sunscreen.

Please call 317-7905 to RSVP by June 10th. Hope you can make it.

Sincerely,

Jackson Preiss

Read the passage aloud. Students should follow along in their books. Then, students should complete the graphic organizer and the writing activity using the prompt on Student Workbook page 85.

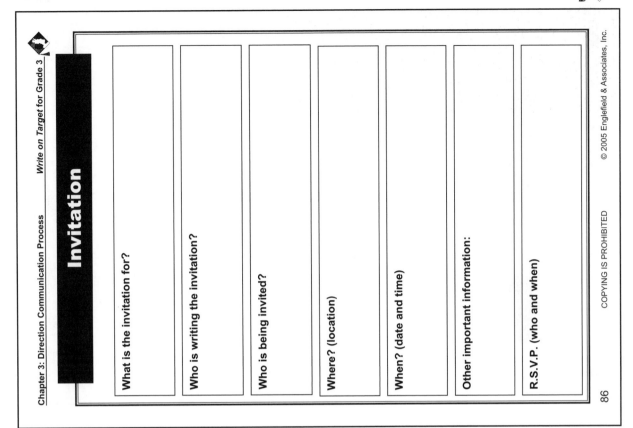

Invitation

What is the invitation for?

Who is writing the invitation?

Who is being invited?

Where? (location)

When? (date and time)

Other important information:

R.S.V.P. (who and when)

Step 2

There are several things to keep in mind as you plan and write your invitation. Remember, a good invitation has the following parts:

- information about where and when to attend
- the type of event or the purpose of the event
- information for an RSVP
- important details about the event

Step 3

Use the following prompt to complete the prewriting and writing activities:

> **Career day is scheduled next month at your school. Write an invitation to someone whom you would like to invite to speak to your class about his or her job. You can invite a local sports figure, a family member, a politician, a business owner, or someone else you think has an interesting career.**

Step 4

Complete the graphic organizer on the next page as your prewriting activity. Use your graphic organizer to help you think through your invitation.

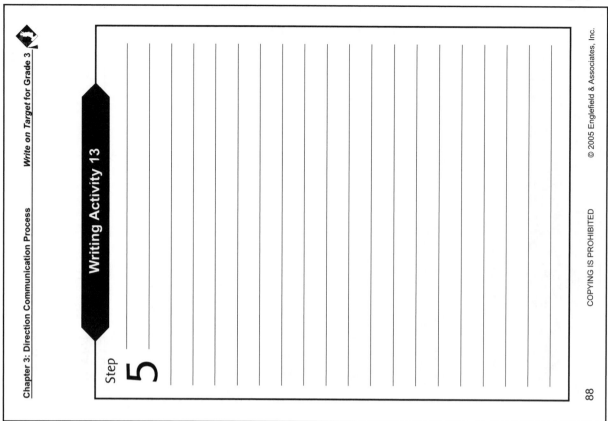

Writing Activity 13

Step

5

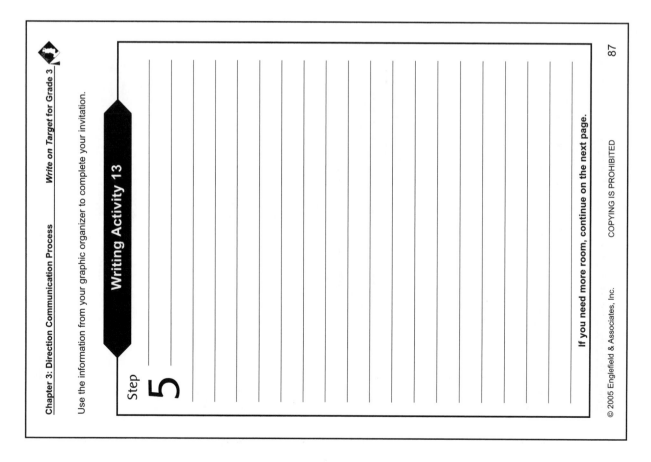

Use the information from your graphic organizer to complete your invitation.

Writing Activity 13

Step

5

If you need more room, continue on the next page.

Notes on Student Responses

Step

6

The checklist shows what your best invitation must include. Use the checklist below to review your work.

Checklist for Writing Activity 13

- ☐ My invitation includes all the important details for my guests such as the type of event, where and when to attend, and RSVP information.

- ☐ I let my guests know why I am inviting them.

- ☐ I try to spell words correctly without using any help.

- ☐ I use interesting words.

- ☐ My sentences and proper names begin with a capital letter.

- ☐ My sentences end with a period, an exclamation point, or a question mark.

- ☐ I have written my invitation so the reader can read my print or cursive writing.

Student Writing Activity 14: An Invitation

Write on Target **for Grade 3**

Step

1

Follow along as the invitation below is read aloud.

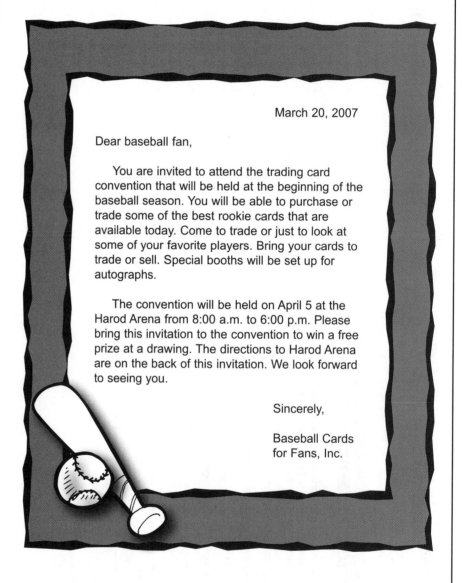

March 20, 2007

Dear baseball fan,

　　You are invited to attend the trading card convention that will be held at the beginning of the baseball season. You will be able to purchase or trade some of the best rookie cards that are available today. Come to trade or just to look at some of your favorite players. Bring your cards to trade or sell. Special booths will be set up for autographs.

　　The convention will be held on April 5 at the Harod Arena from 8:00 a.m. to 6:00 p.m. Please bring this invitation to the convention to win a free prize at a drawing. The directions to Harod Arena are on the back of this invitation. We look forward to seeing you.

Sincerely,

Baseball Cards
for Fans, Inc.

Read the passage aloud. Students should follow along in their books. Then, students should complete the graphic organizer and the writing activity using the prompt on Student Workbook page 91.

Invitation

What is the invitation for?

Who is writing the invitation?

Who is being invited?

Where? (location)

When? (date and time)

Other important information:

R.S.V.P. (who and when)

COPYING IS PROHIBITED   92

Step 2

There are several things to keep in mind as you plan and write your invitation. Remember, a good invitation has the following parts:

- information about where and when to attend
- the type of event or the purpose of the event
- information for an RSVP
- important details about the event

Step 3

Use the following prompt to complete the prewriting and writing activities:

> **Your school is sponsoring a book fair to raise money to buy more books for the school's library. Write an invitation to the parents of the students in your school so they will know about the book fair.**

Step 4

Complete the graphic organizer on the next page as your prewriting activity. Use your graphic organizer to help you think through your invitation.

91

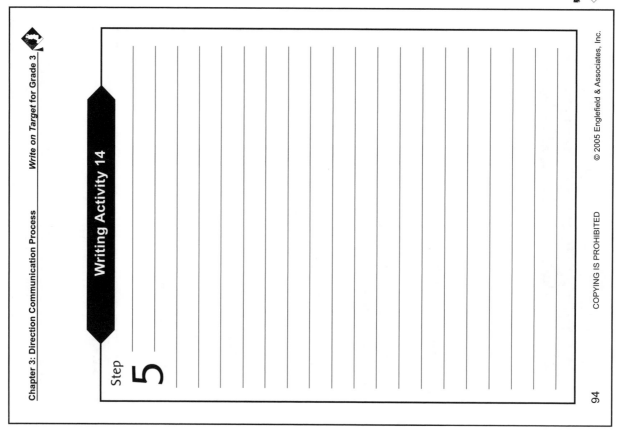

Writing Activity 14

Step

5

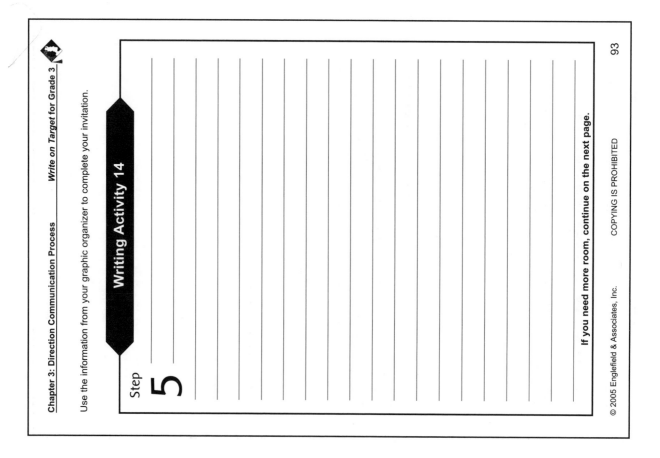

Use the information from your graphic organizer to complete your invitation.

Writing Activity 14

Step

5

If you need more room, continue on the next page.

Notes on Student Responses

Step

6

The checklist shows what your best invitation must include. Use the checklist below to review your work.

Checklist for Writing Activity 14

☐ My invitation includes all the important details for my guests such as the type of event, where and when to attend, and RSVP information.

☐ I let my guests know why I am inviting them.

☐ I try to spell words correctly without using any help.

☐ I use interesting words.

☐ My sentences and proper names begin with a capital letter.

☐ My sentences end with a period, an exclamation point, or a question mark.

☐ I have written my invitation so the reader can read my print or cursive writing.

Additional Writing Prompts for Directions on How to Do Something

1. Explain to someone how to make a smoothie or a milkshake.

2. Explain to someone how to order a pizza.

3. Explain to someone how to microwave popcorn.

4. Explain to someone how to log on to your computer.

5. Explain to someone how to play your favorite board game or card game.

6. Explain to someone how to make your favorite recipe.

Additional Prompts for Directions on How to Go Somewhere or How to Find Something

1. Tell someone how to find a telephone number in the phone book.

2. Tell someone how to select an interesting book at the library.

3. Give someone directions from your classroom to the principal's office, playground, gym, or lunchroom.

Additional Writing Prompts for an Invitation

1. Invite someone to join your girl scout or boy scout troop.

2. Invite a nurse or a doctor to discuss a health issue.

3. Invite someone to a school's open house.

4. Invite someone to make a special treat with you.

5. Invite someone to a skating party.

6. Invite someone to a holiday party.

4 The Explanation Communication Process

(Thank-You Note, Summary, and Informational Report)

The purposes of this chapter include:

1 Showing how the explanation communication process links to the writing modes.

2 Discussing the purpose and features of an informational report, a summary, and a thank-you note.

3 Providing teaching tips on where students break down during the explanation process.

4 Providing ideas for the development of additional writing prompts for an informational report, a summary, and a thank-you note.

> The following teaching tools will be provided for an **informational report**, a **summary**, and a **thank-you note**: a graphic organizer, two writing prompts, and student checklists.

What is the Explanation Communication Process?

Explanation is a communication process that appears across all subject areas in the curriculum. The purpose of explanation is for the writer to give reasons why something occurred.

For an explanation, the writer gives a reason or an opinion with a justification; he or she must be able to provide facts with supporting details. An explanation may require the ability to infer (e.g., Why do you think the character felt that way?). Oftentimes, an explanation requires the ability to use only information given in a selection to support the explanation (e.g., Use information from the selection to support your answer.). Understanding cause and effect is important to the explanation process (e.g., This happened because…).

Features of the Thank-You Note

- Written in letter format with date, greeting, body, closing, and signature

- Explains why the writer is thankful for something done for or given to him or her

Features of an Informational Report

- Nonfiction writing about a person, place, thing, or event

- Provides information about some or all of the following questions:

What or who is it?	Where is it?
What does it look like?	When is it?
What does it do?	Why is it important?

Features of a Summary (Only the Important Information)

- The main idea is identified.

- Supporting details are not included.

- Trivial and redundant information is not included.

- Similar facts, ideas, and information are grouped across paragraphs.

- Only the information essential to complete the communication is conveyed.

- The summary is shorter in length than the original.

- A summary is told in the student's own words.

Correlation of Explanation Communication to the Writing Modes

Informational Report – a piece of nonfiction writing that is based on researched facts, but is written in the student's own words. It is presented in an organized format with a beginning, a middle, and an end. It can cover a wide variety of topics. The purpose of an informational piece of writing is to inform the reader about what the author has learned.

Summary – a piece of writing identifying the topic of the text selection. A summary states the main ideas of the text selection. It does not include information that is not important. A summary has fewer details than retellings.

Thank-You Note – a piece of writing that is written in the form of a letter and includes a date, a greeting, a body, a closing, and a signature. A thank-you note explains what the writer is thankful for and why.

Teaching Tips: Where Students Break Down in the Explanation Communication Process

In general, students have difficulty:

- Understanding when to infer and when to use the selection to make their points. (Example: Students are asked to use ONLY the text selection to provide evidence for their opinions or statements, or students are asked to explain their own opinions, conclusions, or observations based on the information provided in the text.)

- Understanding the relationship between cause and effect.

- Using facts and supporting details.

- Distinguishing between facts and opinions in the selection.

Informational Report

- Students have difficulty organizing the information in a logical order.

- Student writers do not provide a closing to the report. The closing should summarize the importance of the ideas presented.

- Some students are unable to pick out the important ideas and eliminate nonessential information.

- Some students have difficulty writing the ideas in their own words.

Summary

- Students have difficulty picking out the main idea especially in paragraphs that do not have topic sentences.

- Students have difficulty eliminating nonessential information.

- Students have difficulty using titles, subheadings, and boldface words to compose their summaries.

Thank-You Note

- Students do not address the reader with an appropriate greeting.

- Students have difficulty explaining or expressing why the gift or favor was appreciated.

Student Writing Activity 15: Informational Report

Step **1**   Follow along as the informational report "Amazing Arachnids" is read aloud.

Amazing Arachnids

According to Greek legends, Arachne was a wonderful weaver of cloth. She challenged the goddess Athena to a weaving contest and won. Athena was very angry, so she turned Arachne into a spider who spent the rest of her life spinning webs. That is how spiders became known as *arachnids*.

Although some people refer to spiders as bugs, they are not insects. Spiders have eight legs, not six like an insect, and have only two body parts. They also do not have wings or antennae. Spiders are incredible creatures. They weave webs that are very beautiful. Spiders can never really see their webs because they have such poor eyesight. Their blood is a pale blue color rather than bright red like the blood found in humans.

Spiders eat insects, other spiders, and some can even eat birds, frogs, fish, or lizards. Many spiders are small and have the ability to hide or blend into their surroundings. Some species of spiders look like leaves or bark. Most spiders live for only one year, but some spiders, like the tarantula, can live up to 20 years.

Spiders spin webs with sticky threads. The shape and size of the spider web varies with the kind of spider. Some are in the shape of a funnel, orb, hammock, or even a tangle of threads. Spiders' silk is one of the strongest materials on earth. A thread of silk created by the spider is stronger than a thread of steel of the same size. Spiders are skillful weavers that know their own webs so well that they never get caught in the strands of silk they spin.

Spiders help mankind by capturing insects. Spiders turn their prey into a liquid pulp and then eat the mush. They can even remove the crunchy part of the insect. Spiders are amazing creatures.

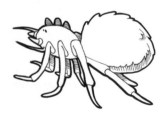

Read the report aloud. Students should follow along in their books. Then, students should complete the graphic organizer and the writing activity using the prompt on Student Workbook page 99.

Step 3

Facts About Fish

- Water covers about 70 percent of Earth.
- There are billions of fish alive today with over 20,000 species.
- Fish can be found in mountain streams, salty oceans, swamps, ponds, lakes, and streams.
- Fish are vertebrates so they have a backbone.
- Most fish breathe oxygen through their gills and have fins and scales.
- Fish use their fins to move through the water.
- Fish are cold-blooded so their body temperature depends on their surroundings.
- Fish have adapted to their surroundings; some live in fresh water while others can only survive in salt water.
- A person who studies fish is known as an ichthyologist.
- Fish eat diatoms, insect larvae, algae, and even turtles and frogs.
- Fish are slimy because they have a special coating that protects them from parasites and disease.
- Birds, snakes, turtles, humans, and other fish feast on fish.

Step 2

There are several things to keep in mind as you plan and write your own informational report. Remember, a good informational report includes the following parts:

- a title
- an explanation of the topic
- only the important information
- a summary of what I have learned

Step 3

Use the following prompt to complete the prewriting and writing activities:

> **Read through the information given about fish on the next page. Use the Information Planning Guide to select and group the information that you will use to create a report that provides the reader with information about fish. Use the information you gather in the planning guide to complete your graphic organizer on page 102. You do not have to use every fact to complete your report. You will need to organize the material and add words of your own.**
>
> **Write a report on fish using "Facts About Fish" on page 100. Use the informational report organizer on page 102 to write an introduction, one to two paragraphs, and a summary that ends your report.**

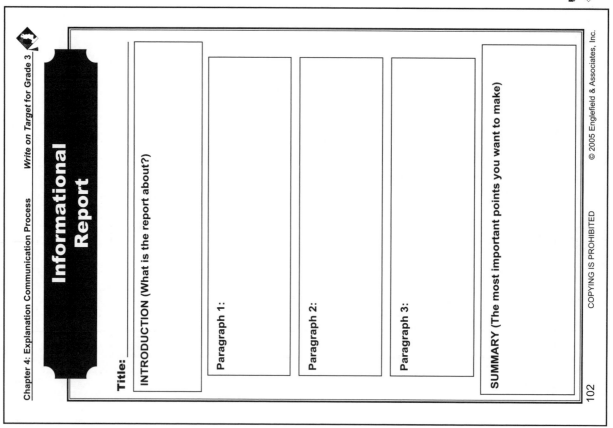

Informational Report

Title: _____

INTRODUCTION (What is the report about?)

Paragraph 1:

Paragraph 2:

Paragraph 3:

SUMMARY (The most important points you want to make)

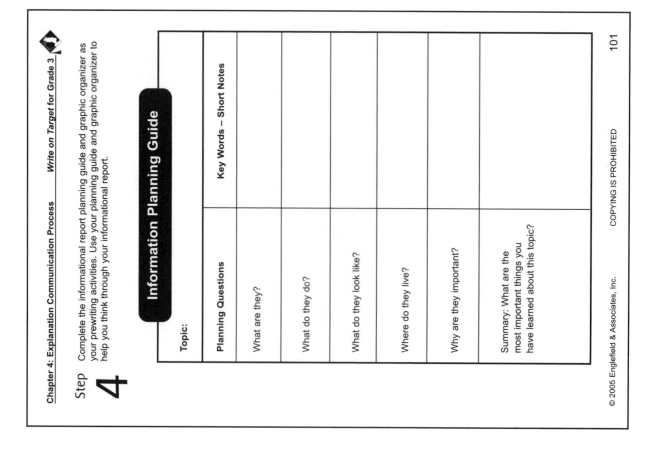

Step 4

Complete the informational report planning guide and graphic organizer as your prewriting activities. Use your planning guide and graphic organizer to help you think through your informational report.

Information Planning Guide

Topic: _____

Planning Questions	Key Words – Short Notes
What are they?	
What do they do?	
What do they look like?	
Where do they live?	
Why are they important?	
Summary: What are the most important things you have learned about this topic?	

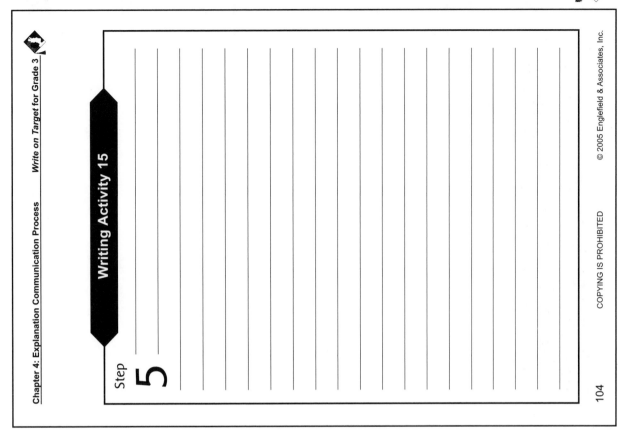

Writing Activity 15

Step **5**

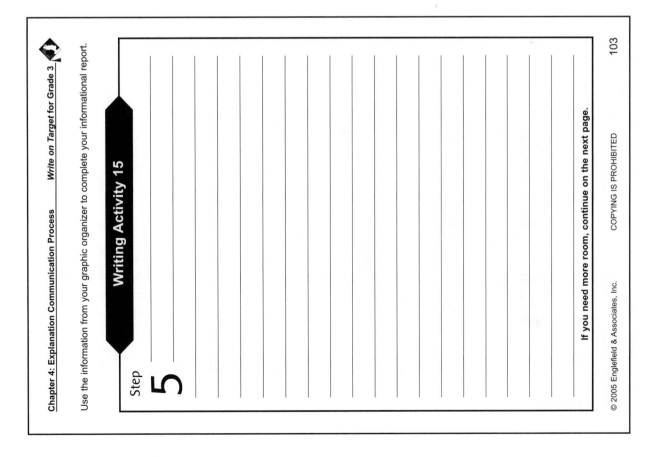

Use the information from your graphic organizer to complete your informational report.

Writing Activity 15

Step **5**

If you need more room, continue on the next page.

Notes on Student Responses

Step

6

The checklist shows what your best informational report must include. Use the checklist below to review your work.

Checklist for Writing Activity 15

☐ My informational report has a title.

☐ My informational report tells the reader the topic of my report.

☐ My report includes only points that are important for readers to know.

☐ My report does not include information that is not important to making my main points.

☐ My report tells the reader what I have learned.

☐ My report has a beginning, middle, and end.

☐ I try to spell words correctly without using any help.

☐ I use interesting words.

☐ My sentences and proper names begin with a capital letter.

☐ My sentences end with a period, an exclamation point, or a question mark.

☐ I have written my report so the reader can read my print or cursive writing.

Student Writing Activity 16: Informational Report

Write on Target for Grade 3

Step 1

Follow along as the informational report "A Woman Who Made a Difference" is read aloud.

A Woman Who Made A Difference

In the past, the lives of women in America were very different than they are today. Women were only allowed to do certain jobs. They were not allowed to attend every school. There was a time when there were no doctors who were women. Today, women in America have better lives with more choices because of determined women like Elizabeth Blackwell.

Elizabeth Blackwell was born in England in 1821. When Elizabeth was 11 years old, her family moved from England to America. In America, just like in England, women couldn't do very much to make money except sew, teach, work as a servant, or work in a factory.

When Elizabeth's father died, her family became poor. Elizabeth needed to decide what she was going to do to make money. Elizabeth visited a sick friend who told Elizabeth that she would be a good doctor. Because of that experience, Elizabeth decided what she wanted to do. She would try to become a doctor. Unfortunately, most medical schools didn't accept women. Twenty-nine schools said no, but Elizabeth kept trying. She was determined and refused to give up.

Finally, Geneva Medical College in New York state said "yes" to Elizabeth. Elizabeth had the best grades and graduated first in her class. She was Doctor Blackwell now, the first woman doctor. Elizabeth wrote books and made speeches. During her life, she fought for female doctors, cleanliness in hospitals, and for better care for poor women and children.

Elizabeth died in England. She was 89 years old. The little girl who became the first woman doctor had done many important things to help change the lives of other people. The lives of women in America and all over the world are better today because of Elizabeth Blackwell.

Read the report aloud. Students should follow along in their books. Then, students should complete the graphic organizer and the writing activity using the prompt on Student Workbook page 107.

Step 3

Facts About Bill Gates

- Bill Gates is one of the richest people in the world.
- Bill Gates started a computer software company called Microsoft in 1975.
- Some people think Bill Gates has not always made business decisions that were fair.
- Bill Gates was born in Seattle, Washington.
- Bill Gates is a philanthropist.
- During the 1980s, the computer industry grew rapidly.
- Bill Gates thought that with computers, people could work faster and communicate with each other more easily.
- A philanthropist is someone who helps people by giving money to worthy causes.
- In 1985, Microsoft introduced the Windows operating system which made personal computers easier to use.
- Bill Gates thought computers could help people in their homes, schools, and offices.
- Bill Gates became a billionaire when he was just 31 years old.
- Paul Allen worked with Bill Gates to start Microsoft.
- Bill Gates likes to donate money to schools, universities, and libraries.

Step 2

There are several things to keep in mind as you plan and write your own informational report. Remember, a good informational report includes the following parts:

- a title
- an explanation of the topic
- only the important information
- a summary of what I have learned

Step 3

Use the following prompt to complete the prewriting and writing activities:

> **Read through the information given about Bill Gates on the next page. Use the Information Planning Guide to select and group the information that you will use to create a report that provides the reader with information about Bill Gates. Use the information you gather in the planning guide to complete your graphic organizer on page 110. You do not have to use every fact to complete your report. You will need to organize the material and add words of your own.**
>
> **Write a report on Bill Gates using "Facts About Bill Gates" on page 108. Use the informational report organizer on page 110 to write an introduction, one to two paragraphs, and a summary that ends your report.**

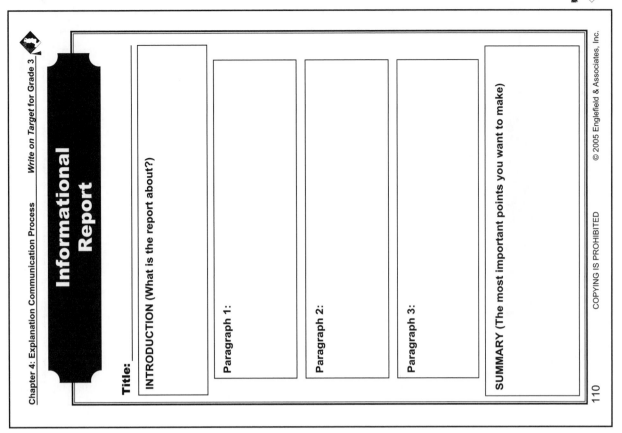

Chapter 4: Explanation Communication Process *Write on Target* for Grade 3

Informational Report

Title: _____

INTRODUCTION (What is the report about?)

Paragraph 1:

Paragraph 2:

Paragraph 3:

SUMMARY (The most important points you want to make)

110   COPYING IS PROHIBITED   © 2005 Englefield & Associates, Inc.

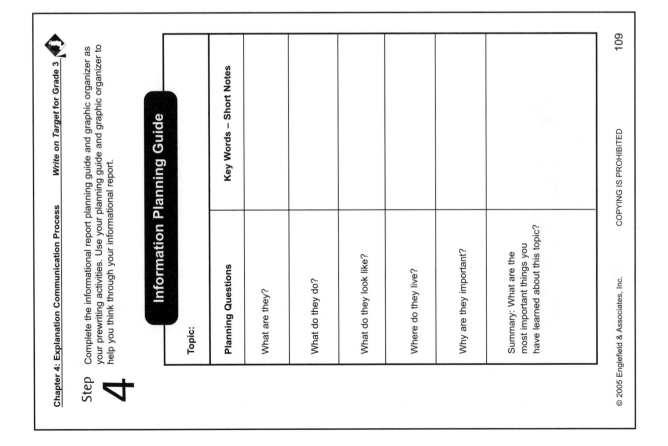

Chapter 4: Explanation Communication Process *Write on Target* for Grade 3

Step 4 Complete the informational report planning guide and graphic organizer as your prewriting activities. Use your planning guide and graphic organizer to help you think through your informational report.

Information Planning Guide

Topic:

Planning Questions	Key Words – Short Notes
What are they?	
What do they do?	
What do they look like?	
Where do they live?	
Why are they important?	
Summary: What are the most important things you have learned about this topic?	

© 2005 Englefield & Associates, Inc.   COPYING IS PROHIBITED   109

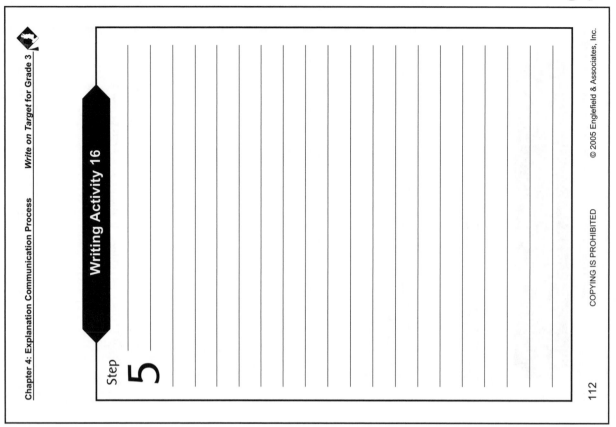

Writing Activity 16

Step 5

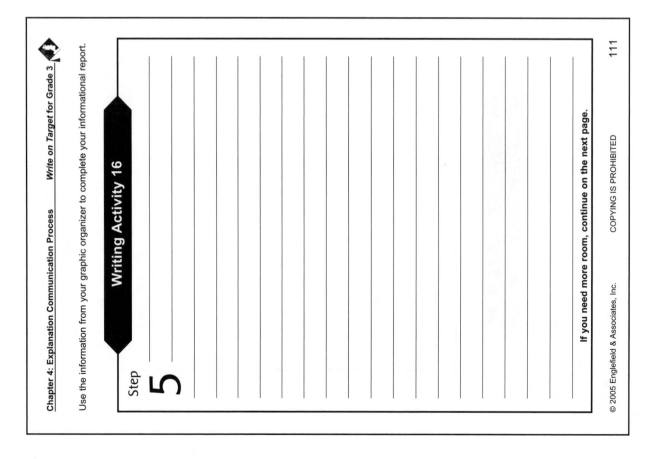

Use the information from your graphic organizer to complete your informational report.

Writing Activity 16

Step 5

If you need more room, continue on the next page.

Notes on Student Responses

Step

6

The checklist shows what your best informational report must include. Use the checklist below to review your work.

Checklist for Writing Activity 16

☐ My informational report has a title.

☐ My informational report tells the reader the topic of my report.

☐ My report includes only points that are important for readers to know.

☐ My report does not include information that is not important to making my main points.

☐ My report tells the reader what I have learned.

☐ My report has a beginning, middle, and end.

☐ I try to spell words correctly without using any help.

☐ I use interesting words.

☐ My sentences and proper names begin with a capital letter.

☐ My sentences end with a period, an exclamation point, or a question mark.

☐ I have written my report so the reader can read my print or cursive writing.

Student Writing Activity 17: Summary

Step 1 Follow along as two passages are read. The first passage is a report titled "Copernicus and His Discovery." The second passage is a summary of "Copernicus and His Discovery."

Copernicus and His Discovery

Today, we know that Earth moves around the sun. More than 500 years ago, however, people believed that Earth was the center of the universe. People thought the sun moved around Earth. One scientist was brave enough to question that belief. His name was Copernicus.

Copernicus was born in Poland in 1473. He studied astronomy in Italy by just using his eyes to study the stars and the planets. Eventually, Copernicus concluded that Earth revolves around the sun. He sent his papers to the leaders of the time.

Copernicus knew that this new way of thinking would not be popular with people of that time because they wanted to think that Earth was important. He made an important discovery about Earth, the sun, and the other planets without even using a telescope.

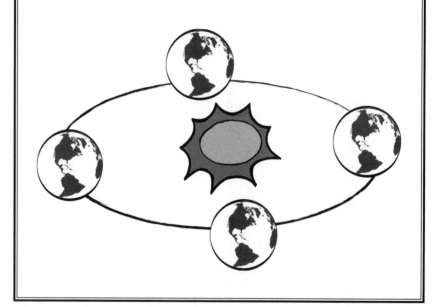

114   COPYING IS PROHIBITED   © 2005 Englefield & Associates, Inc.

Read the passage and the summary aloud. Students should follow along in their books. Then, students should complete the graphic organizer and the writing activity using the prompt on Student Workbook page 116.

Step

1

Summary of "Copernicus and His Discovery"

Over 500 years ago, the Polish astronomer Copernicus discovered that Earth moves around the sun. Without the use of a telescope, he studied the stars and the planets. His discovery was not popular because people wanted to believe that Earth was the important planet and that the sun moved around Earth. Copernicus changed the way we view Earth.

115

Read the summary aloud. Students should follow along in their books. Then, students should complete the graphic organizer and the writing activity using the prompt on Student Workbook page 116.

99

Step 3

"Mr. Watson, Come Here"

Can you imagine not being able to talk on the telephone? Alexander Graham Bell was born in 1847 to parents who worked with deaf children. He was interested in how sound traveled even when he was a young boy. At that time, people could only communicate by writing a letter or sending a telegram using Morse code.

When he was young, he made a simple phone of tin and rubber. Later, he designed a machine with a transmitter that turned sounds into electricity that traveled through wire. He then created a receiver that turned signals back into sounds.

On March 1876, he spoke the first words through his telephone: "Mr. Watson, come here, I want to see you."

Thomas Watson, who was in the next room, could hear the words clearly. At the American Centennial Convention in Philadelphia, Bell won a prize for inventors.

He invented many other objects, including the phonograph record, the x-ray machine, and a special kite. Alexander Graham Bell will always be remembered as the inventor of the telephone.

Step 2

There are several things to keep in mind as you plan to write a summary. Remember, a good summary:

- includes the main ideas
- eliminates unimportant or unnecessary information
- does not include many details
- is written in your own words

Step 3

Use the following prompt to complete the prewriting and writing activities:

Read the story "Mr. Watson, Come Here" on page 117 and write a summary.

Step 4

Complete the graphic organizer on page 118 as your prewriting activity. Use your graphic organizer to help you think through your summary of "Mr. Watson, Come Here."

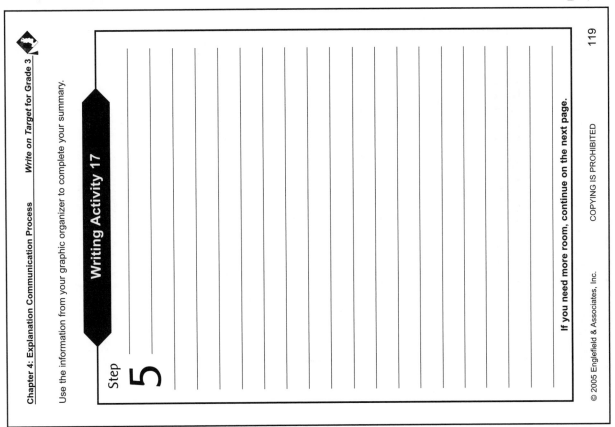

Use the information from your graphic organizer to complete your summary.

Writing Activity 17

Step 5

If you need more room, continue on the next page.

119

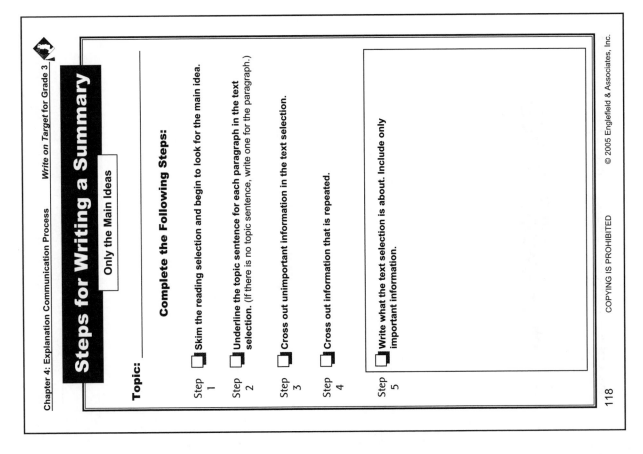

Steps for Writing a Summary

Only the Main Ideas

Topic:

Complete the Following Steps:

Step 1   Skim the reading selection and begin to look for the main idea.

Step 2   Underline the topic sentence for each paragraph in the text selection. (If there is no topic sentence, write one for the paragraph.)

Step 3   Cross out unimportant information in the text selection.

Step 4   Cross out information that is repeated.

Step 5   Write what the text selection is about. Include only important information.

118

Step 6

The checklist shows what your best summary must include. Use the checklist below to review your work.

Checklist for Writing Activity 17

☐ My summary has a sentence that identifies the topic of the text selection.

☐ My summary states the main ideas of the text selection.

☐ My summary does not include information that is not important to the story.

☐ My summary has an ending.

☐ I try to spell words correctly without using any help.

☐ I use interesting words.

☐ My sentences and proper names begin with a capital letter.

☐ My sentences end with a period, an exclamation point, or a question mark.

☐ I have written my summary so the reader can read my print or cursive writing.

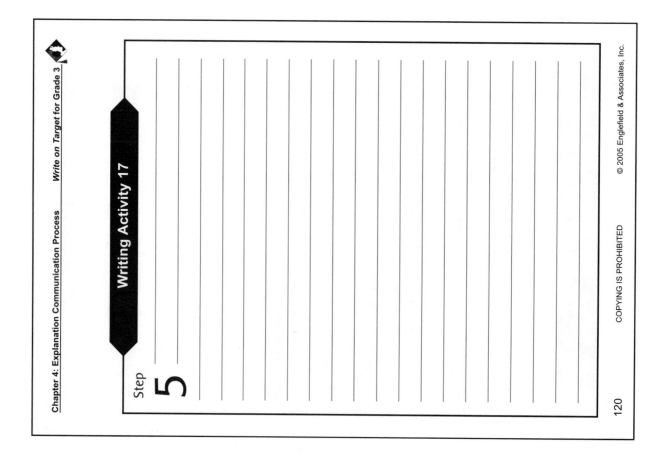

Step 5

Writing Activity 17

Student Writing Activity 18: Summary

Step 1 Follow along as two passages are read. The first passage is a report titled "Now You See Them, Now You Don't." The second passage is a summary of "Now You See Them, Now You Don't."

Now You See Them, Now You Don't

Have you ever tried to hide from someone? Sometimes it's hard to find a good place to hide. Just think—if you could blend in with your surroundings, you would be much harder to find.

The word *camouflage* means something is hidden because it blends in with its surroundings. Being camouflaged is a disguise. Animals, fish, reptiles, and even people use camouflage for hiding.

There are many reasons for animals to hide. They often hide from their enemies. An animal has less of a chance of being eaten if it is the same color as the things around it. Some animals move around at night and sleep during the day. They need to stay hidden while they sleep. Other animals need to be able to hide so they can be better hunters. Camouflage helps them sneak up on their dinner.

When the surrounding world changes color, certain animals change, too. For example, a white hare is difficult for a wolf to see in the white snow. In the spring, when the snow melts, the hare will still be hard to see because its fur turns light brown and blends in with the brown colors of the woods. A type of lizard called a chameleon can quickly change its color to match its surroundings. A green insect on a green leaf is hard for a hungry frog to see. Some insects are even shaped like sticks or leaves. These insects blend in not only with the colors around them, but with the shapes, too.

People sometimes use camouflage, too. Think about the clothing hunters and soldiers in the military wear. They usually wear clothes that help them blend in with their surroundings. Most likely, these people got the idea for camouflage from animals.

122   COPYING IS PROHIBITED   © 2005 Englefield & Associates, Inc.

Read the passage and the summary aloud. Students should follow along in their books. Then, students should complete the graphic organizer and the writing activity using the prompt on Student Workbook page 124.

Step

1

Summary of "Now You See Them, Now You Don't"

When something is camouflaged, that means it blends in with its surroundings and is hidden. Animals, fish, reptiles, and even people sometimes use camouflage to hide.

Animals hide from their enemies so they won't be eaten. They also hide so they can sleep or sneak up on their prey. Some animals change colors when the seasons change. The white hare has white fur when it snows and brown fur when the snow melts. Its fur hides it in the landscape. Some insects are camouflaged by being shaped like sticks or leaves.

People can camouflage themselves, too. Hunters and soldiers wear camouflaged clothing so they can't be seen.

Read the summary aloud. Students should follow along in their books. Then, students should complete the graphic organizer and the writing activity using the prompt on Student Workbook page 124.

Step 3

The Garden

Mishka's father enjoyed being outdoors. Every spring, he would spend hours in the yard planting his garden. First, he would till the soil with a tiller to loosen it. Then, he would plant corn, tomatoes, and squash.

One afternoon, Mishka arrived home from school before his father was home from work. He loved his father and wanted to do something to make him happy. He looked out his window and saw the garden. He thought about how happy his father would be if Mishka weeded the garden. It would be a surprise! So, that is what Mishka decided to do.

Mishka ran right outside and started pulling weed after weed. When he finished, he couldn't wait for his father to arrive home to see what he had done. He was so excited! Finally, his father came home. Mishka grabbed his father's hand and pulled him out of the house to see the garden.

Mishka's father looked at the garden and said, "Mishka, what have you done? Where are all of the vegetable plants?" Mishka's heart sank. He realized he had pulled out the vegetable plants and left the weeds. Mishka burst into tears. His father looked at him. He bent down and gave Mishka a hug. He said, "Mishka, it's going to be OK. We can replant the vegetables. They haven't been out of the ground for very long. The roots are not dried out, so they will still grow."

Mishka and his father replanted the vegetables that day. Mishka's father said he understood that Mishka wanted to do something to make him happy. He told Mishka that he loved him and didn't want him to worry about this mistake anymore. Over the next few months, the vegetables grew. Before long, Mishka and his father were eating those beautiful vegetables.

Step 2

There are several things to keep in mind as you plan to write a summary. Remember, a good summary:

· includes the main ideas

· eliminates unimportant or unnecessary information

· does not include many details

· is written in your own words

Step 3

Use the following prompt to complete the prewriting and writing activities:

Read the story "The Garden" on page 125 and write a summary.

Step 4

Complete the graphic organizer on page 126 as your prewriting activity. Use your graphic organizer to help you think through your summary of "The Garden."

Use the information from your graphic organizer to complete your summary.

Writing Activity 18

Step 5

If you need more room, continue on the next page.

127

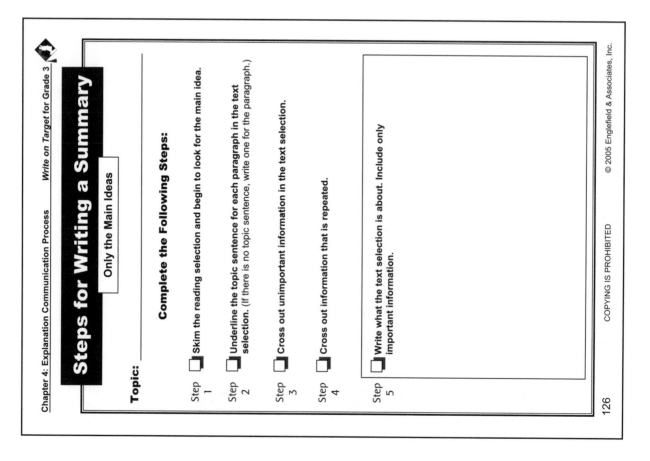

Steps for Writing a Summary

Only the Main Ideas

Topic: _____

Complete the Following Steps:

☐ **Step 1** — **Skim the reading selection and begin to look for the main idea.**

☐ **Step 2** — **Underline the topic sentence for each paragraph in the text selection.** (If there is no topic sentence, write one for the paragraph.)

☐ **Step 3** — **Cross out unimportant information in the text selection.**

☐ **Step 4** — **Cross out information that is repeated.**

☐ **Step 5** — **Write what the text selection is about. Include only important information.**

126

Step 6

The checklist shows what your best summary must include. Use the checklist below to review your work.

Checklist for Writing Activity 18

☐ My summary has a sentence that identifies the topic of the text selection.

☐ My summary states the main ideas of the text selection.

☐ My summary does not include information that is not important to the story.

☐ My summary has an ending.

☐ I try to spell words correctly without using any help.

☐ I use interesting words.

☐ My sentences and proper names begin with a capital letter.

☐ My sentences end with a period, an exclamation point, or a question mark.

☐ I have written my summary so the reader can read my print or cursive writing.

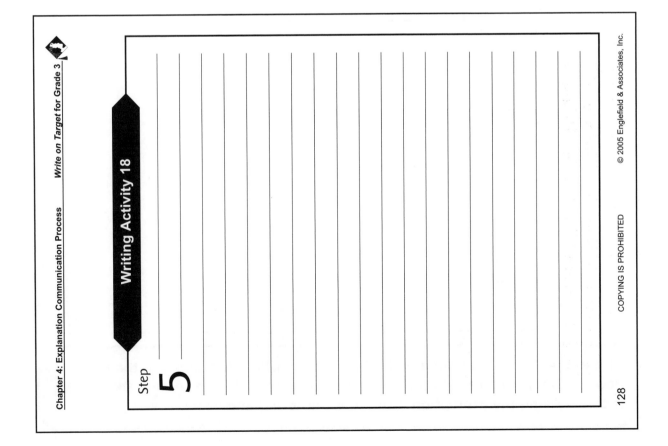

Writing Activity 18

Step 5

Student Writing Activity 19: Thank-You Note

Step

1

Follow along as the thank-you note below is read aloud.

November 2, 2007

Dear Mr. Williams,

  Thank you for coming to our classroom and showing us your fossil collection. I especially liked the fossil snails that you taught us were called ammonites. I thought that it was fun when you had us guess how the fossils might have been formed millions of years ago. I think a meteor might have fallen on a school of fish for one of your fossils. You helped us learn about fossils, which are very interesting. I am thinking that I might like to be a paleontologist like you.

  Thank you for visiting our class. I hope you can come again next year and show more students your exciting fossils.

Your student friend,

Kaylana

> **Read the thank-you note aloud. Students should follow along in their books. Then, students should complete the graphic organizer and the writing activity using the prompt on Student Workbook page 131.**

Thank-You Note

Date:

Greeting or Salutation:

Body—What you are thankful for and why:

Closing:

Signature:

Step 2

There are several things to keep in mind as you plan to write your own thank-you note. Remember, a good thank-you note has the following parts:

- the date
- a greeting or salutation
- a body
- a closing
- a signature

Step 3

Use the following prompt to complete the prewriting and writing activities:

> Write a thank-you note to someone you know who has helped your school or the students in the school in some way. You can thank someone who works at your school, volunteers at your school, or donates money or other items to your school.

Step 4

Complete the graphic organizer on the next page as your prewriting activity. Use your graphic organizer to help you think through your thank-you note.

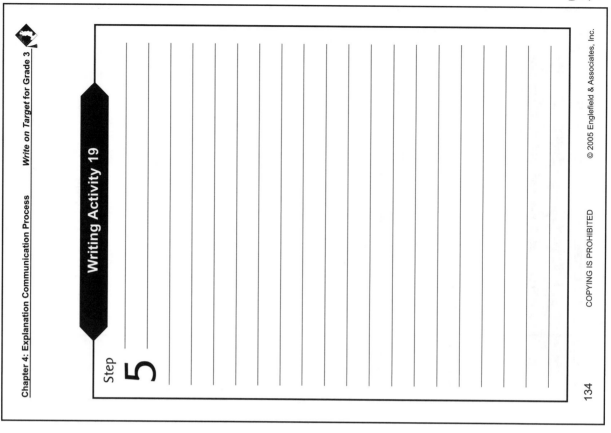

Writing Activity 19

Step

5

134

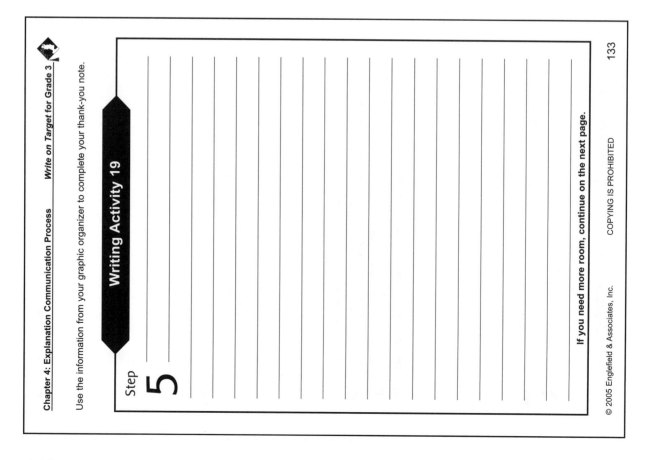

Use the information from your graphic organizer to complete your thank-you note.

Writing Activity 19

Step

5

If you need more room, continue on the next page.

133

Notes on Student Responses

Step

6

The checklist shows what your best thank-you note must include. Use the checklist below to review your work.

Checklist for Writing Activity 19

☐ I use the form for a letter with the date, a greeting, a body, a closing, and a signature.

☐ My thank-you note tells my reader why I am writing and makes a personal comment.

☐ My thank-you note tells why I am thankful using some or all of the following words: looks like, sounds like, does, makes other people feel, makes me feel.

☐ My thank-you note includes a personal closing comment.

☐ I try to spell words correctly without using any help.

☐ I use interesting words.

☐ My sentences and proper names begin with a capital letter.

☐ My sentences end with a period, an exclamation point, or a question mark.

☐ I have written my thank-you note so the reader can read my print or cursive writing.

Student Writing Activity 20: Thank-You Note

Write on Target for Grade 3

Step

1

Follow along as the thank-you note below is read aloud.

June 20, 2006

Dear Ms. Floyd,

Now that the school year is over, I want to thank you for being the best bus driver I have ever had. Every morning when I got on the bus, you greeted me with a big smile and a warm "Good Morning." You were always kind to me. On the mornings when I was running a little bit late, you would wait for me as I was running to catch the bus. I always felt safe when you were driving our bus. I hope you are my bus driver again next year.

Sincerely,

Sam Crosby

Read the thank-you note aloud. Students should follow along in their books. Then, students should complete the graphic organizer and the writing activity using the prompt on Student Workbook page 137.

Thank-You Note

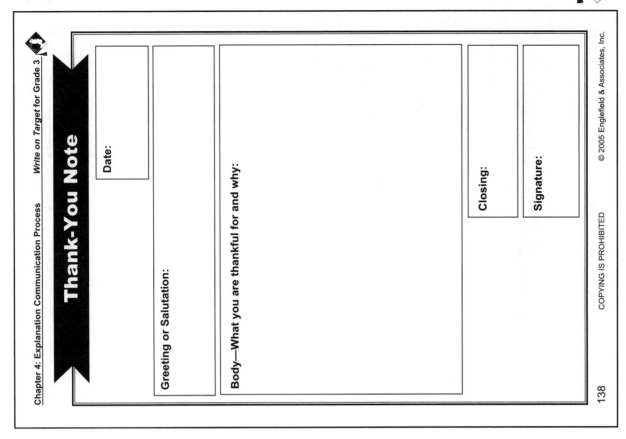

Date:

Greeting or Salutation:

Body—What you are thankful for and why:

Closing:

Signature:

138

Step 2

There are several things to keep in mind as you plan to write your own thank-you note. Remember, a good thank-you note has the following parts:

- the date
- a greeting or salutation
- a body
- a closing
- a signature

Step 3

Use the following prompt to complete the prewriting and writing activities:

> **Write a thank-you note to someone you want to thank for something they have done for you, given to you, or said to you. You can write to anyone. You could write to a family member, a neighbor, a community member, a sports star, or a government official.**

Step 4

Complete the graphic organizer on the next page as your prewriting activity. Use your graphic organizer to help you think through your thank-you note.

137

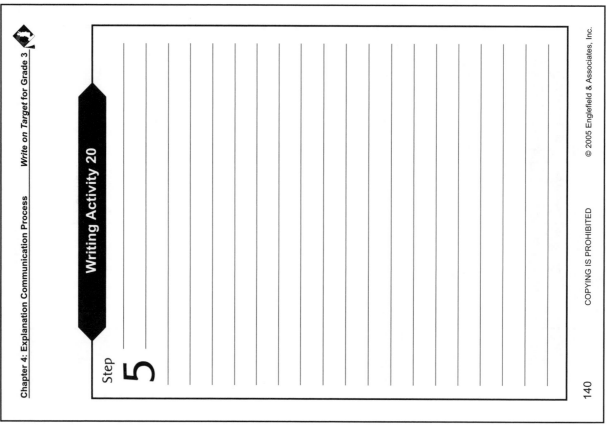

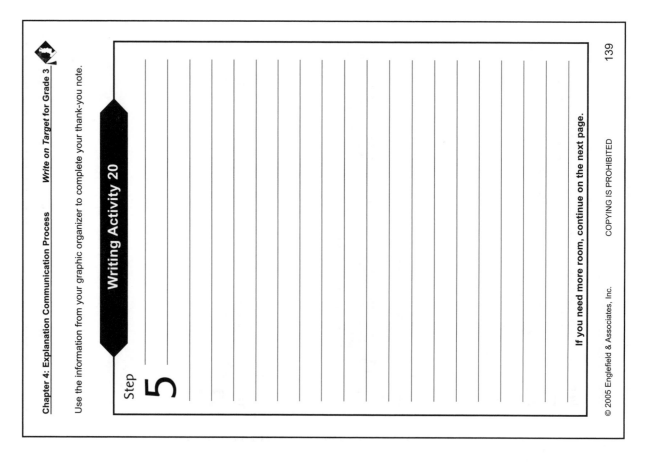

Use the information from your graphic organizer to complete your thank-you note.

If you need more room, continue on the next page.

Notes on Student Responses

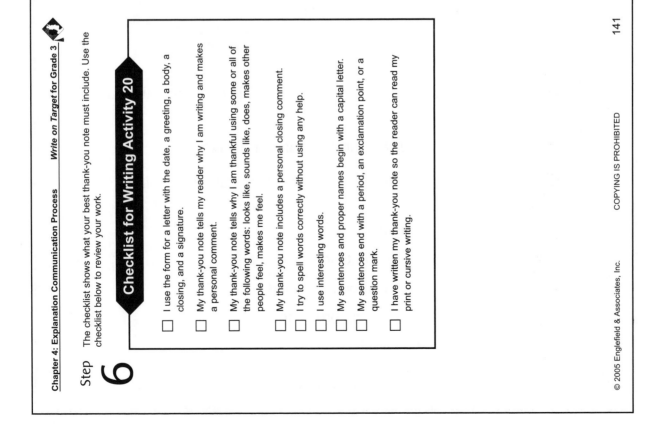

The checklist shows what your best thank-you note must include. Use the checklist below to review your work.

Step 6

Checklist for Writing Activity 20

☐ I use the form for a letter with the date, a greeting, a body, a closing, and a signature.

☐ My thank-you note tells my reader why I am writing and makes a personal comment.

☐ My thank-you note tells why I am thankful using some or all of the following words: looks like, sounds like, does, makes other people feel, makes me feel.

☐ My thank-you note includes a personal closing comment.

☐ I try to spell words correctly without using any help.

☐ I use interesting words.

☐ My sentences and proper names begin with a capital letter.

☐ My sentences end with a period, an exclamation point, or a question mark.

☐ I have written my thank-you note so the reader can read my print or cursive writing.

Additional Writing Prompts for an Informational Report

Write a report on a(n):

- animal
- author
- historical figure
- current event
- historical event
- place you would like to visit
- famous person

Additional Writing Prompts for a Summary

Write a summary of:

- your day at school
- a movie
- a television program
- a sporting event
- a book that you enjoyed
- a field trip
- a funny thing that happened at school or on the playground or the bus

Additional Writing Prompts for a Thank-You Note

Write a thank-you note explaining why you were thankful for the gift or kindness you received:

<u>gift</u>	<u>kindness</u>
• clothing	• presentation to your class
• books	• classroom volunteer
• toys	• field trip presenter
• software	• friend
• a fun trip	

5 The Persuasive Communication Process

(Letter to the Editor)

The purposes of this chapter include:

1   Discussing the purpose and features of a letter to the editor.

2   Showing how the persuasive communication process links to the eleven writing modes.

3   Offering teaching tips on where students break down in the persuasive process.

4   Providing ideas for the development of additional writing prompts for persuasive letters.

> The following teaching tools are provided for **letters to the editor**: graphic organizers, models, two writing prompts, and student checklists.

What is the Persuasive Communication Process?

The purpose of persuasion is to influence another person's or group's thinking about a particular issue. Persuasive techniques can be observed in letters to the editor, advertising campaigns, and speeches.

Features of a Letter to the Editor

- The writer must state his or her position on an issue.

- The writer must provide supporting evidence or reasons for the position taken.

- The reasons should be logical and based on facts (not opinion).

- The writer must anticipate and acknowledge the other side's point of view.

Language of Persuasion

It is my belief that…	On the other hand	What is your point?
In my opinion…	State	However
As noted…	Opinion	Yet
As you can see…	I see your point	I doubt
In conclusion…	For these reasons	Argue
Pro	Point of view	Con

Correlation of Persuasive Communication to the Writing Modes

Letter to the Editor – a piece of writing in the form of a letter, including a date, a greeting, a body, a closing, and a signature that expresses the writer's opinion and why it is important. The writer's opinion should be based on facts, examples, and/or reasons. The writer should also include what he/she would like to see happen.

Teaching Tips: Where Students Break Down in the Persuasive Communication Process

- Students do not understand the difference between fact and opinion.

- Students fail to recognize that there can be a variety of possible positions; there is rarely one "right" position.

- The reasons that students give to influence somebody else's thinking are just personal opinions and are not based on facts.

- Some students are unable to see the position from the other side's point of view.

- Students do not have enough information to argue a position.

Student Writing Activity 21: Letter to the Editor

Write on Target for Grade 3

Step 1 Follow along as the letter to the editor below is read aloud.

April 12, 2007

Dear Editor,

I am writing about an idea I heard about that might help our community. I think our community should start a community vegetable garden.

A community garden would benefit our community in many ways. The garden could be grown on land in our community that needs to be cleaned up. With a garden, the location would get cleaned up and be used for a good purpose. Because a garden would benefit so many people, we might be able to use the land for free. The garden could be run by anyone who wants to participate.

We would invite and welcome everyone to help in the garden. That includes the elderly, the handicapped, teenagers, children, and people of different religions, races, and genders. It would be a wonderful place for people to work together and meet each other.

We have many people in our community who need food, and the vegetables could go to those in need. Our vegetables could be used to feed people.

I hope you will publish my letter. I would like people who want to help me start a community garden to contact me.

Sincerely,

Raul Angelo

Read the letter aloud. Students should follow along in their books. Then, students should complete the graphic organizer and the writing activity using the prompt on Student Workbook page 145.

119

Page 146

Letter to the Editor

Date:

Greeting:

Personal comment (include why you are writing):

Details

First:

Second:

Third:

Personal comments ending the letter (include a restatement of why you are writing):

Closing:

Signature:

Page 145

Step 2

There are several things to keep in mind as you plan and write your own letter to the editor. Remember, a good letter to the editor has the following parts:

- the date, a greeting, a body, a closing, and a signature
- a statement of your opinion
- support for your opinion with facts and statements
- a conclusion that restates your opinion; it may include a suggestion for what needs to be done

Step 3

Use the following prompt to complete the prewriting and writing activities:

> **Write a letter to a newspaper or magazine that people in your community read. Let them know about an idea you have to improve the community.**

Step 4

Complete the graphic organizer on the next page as your prewriting activity. Use your graphic organizer to help you think through your letter to the editor.

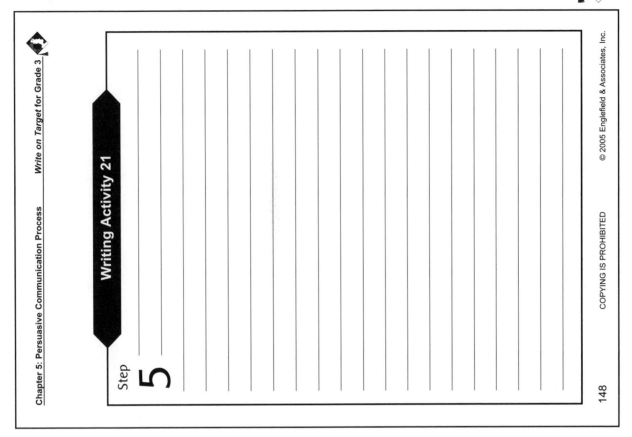

Writing Activity 21

Step

5

148

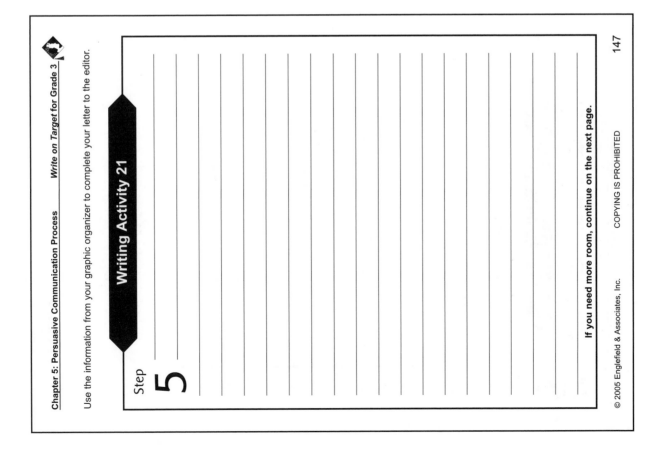

Use the information from your graphic organizer to complete your letter to the editor.

Writing Activity 21

Step

5

If you need more room, continue on the next page.

147

Notes on Student Responses

Chapter 5: Persuasive Communication Process   *Write on Target* **for Grade 3**

Step

6

The checklist shows what your best letter to the editor must include. Use the checklist below to review your work.

Checklist for Writing Activity 21

☐ My persuasive letter tells why I am writing this letter to the editor.

☐ My letter tells why I believe my opinion or information is important.

☐ I state my opinion with facts and examples or important reasons.

☐ I restate my opinion in my conclusion and say what I would like to happen.

☐ I use the form for a letter with a date, a greeting, a body, a closing, and a signature.

☐ I do not use the same words over and over again.

☐ I try to spell words correctly without using any help.

☐ I use interesting words.

☐ My sentences and proper names begin with a capital letter.

☐ My sentences end with a period, an exclamation point, or a question mark.

☐ I have written my letter so that the reader can read my print or cursive writing.

Student Writing Activity 22: Letter to the Editor

Write on Target for Grade 3

Step 1 Follow along as the letter to the editor below is read aloud.

March 23, 2007

Dear Stark Elementary School Students,

I am writing this letter to the students of Stark Elementary School to discuss the littering problem in our school. Our principal, Mrs. Stoddard, has asked the students to take greater pride in our school's halls and grounds. She announced that over three garbage bags of trash are collected every day just in the halls of our school. All of us will need to take responsibility to stop the littering.

Trash in the halls is not what we want visitors to see when they enter our school. The wads of paper, broken pencils, and food wrappers take away from the appearance of our school. There are trash cans located throughout the school, so why not make the effort to use them? We want our halls to be clean.

We students need to become responsible citizens. Littering causes harm to animals, creeks and streams, and our roads. We want our community to be a clean and healthy place. Learning that kind of citizenship begins at school.

The next time that you have a paper cup or broken pencil in your hand, think about putting it in the trash instead of dropping it on the floor. If you see a piece of litter on the floor, pick it up and throw it away. Our school will be a better place, and we all will enjoy our clean building.

Let's remind each other of our responsibility to Stark Elementary School.

Sincerely,

Randy Slade

> **Read the letter aloud. Students should follow along in their books. Then, students should complete the graphic organizer and the writing activity using the prompt on Student Workbook page 151.**

Top section (page 152)

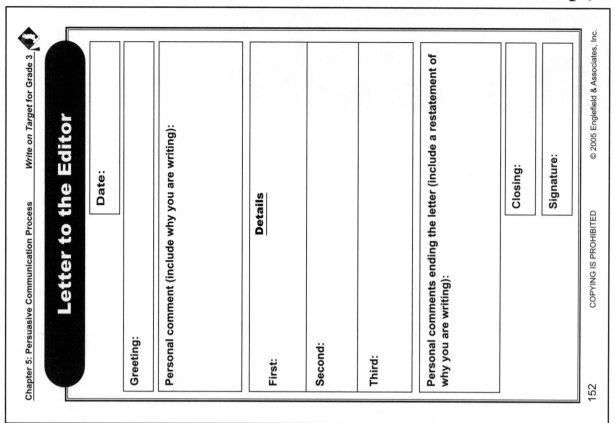

Letter to the Editor

Date:

Greeting:

Personal comment (include why you are writing):

Details

First:

Second:

Third:

Personal comments ending the letter (include a restatement of why you are writing):

Closing:

Signature:

Bottom section (page 151)

Step 2

There are several things to keep in mind as you plan and write your own letter to the editor. Remember, a good letter to the editor has the following parts:

- the date, a greeting, a body, a closing, and a signature
- a statement of your opinion
- support for your opinion with facts and statements
- a conclusion that restates your opinion; it may include a suggestion for what needs to be done

Step 3

Use the following prompt to complete the prewriting and writing activities:

> Think about one thing you feel needs to be changed by students in your school. Think about how you would persuade others to agree to the change. Write a letter to the school's newspaper so that students will understand why the change would be good for everyone.

Step 4

Complete the graphic organizer on the next page as your prewriting activity. Use your graphic organizer to help you think through your letter to the editor.

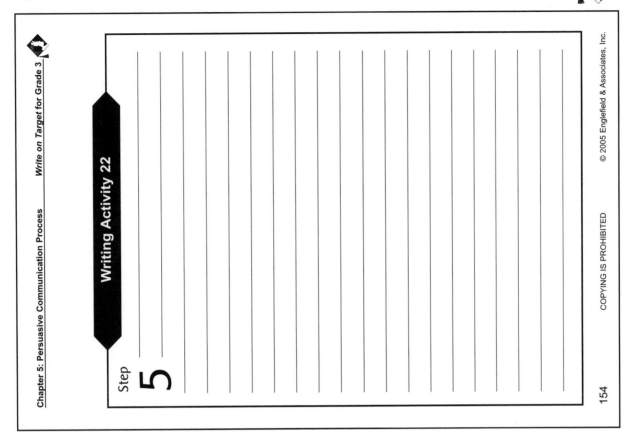

Writing Activity 22

Step **5**

154

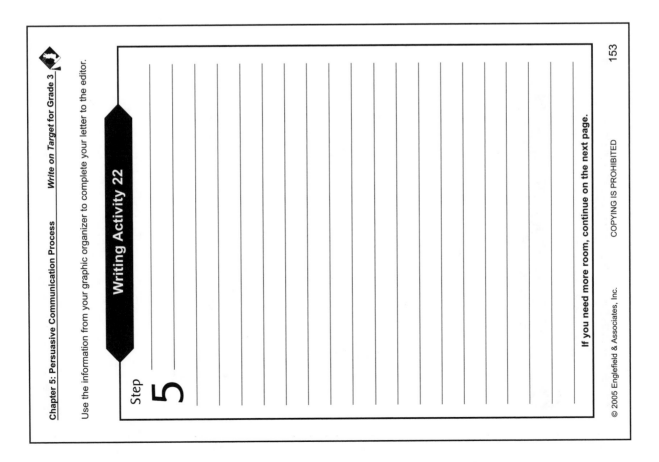

Use the information from your graphic organizer to complete your letter to the editor.

Writing Activity 22

Step **5**

If you need more room, continue on the next page.

153

Notes on Student Responses

Step

6

The checklist shows what your best letter to the editor must include. Use the checklist below to review your work.

Checklist for Writing Activity 22

☐ My persuasive letter tells why I am writing this letter to the editor.

☐ My letter tells why I believe my opinion or information is important.

☐ I state my opinion with facts and examples or important reasons.

☐ I restate my opinion in my conclusion and say what I would like to happen.

☐ I use the form for a letter with a date, a greeting, a body, a closing, and a signature.

☐ I do not use the same words over and over again.

☐ I try to spell words correctly without using any help.

☐ I use interesting words.

☐ My sentences and proper names begin with a capital letter.

☐ My sentences end with a period, an exclamation point, or a question mark.

☐ I have written my letter so that the reader can read my print or cursive writing.

Additional Writing Prompts for a Letter to the Editor

1. School buses should (or should not) have seat belts.

2. Something is needed to improve the school: playground equipment, classroom supplies, more computers, more books, etc.

3. A school rule that should be changed is _____.

4. Changes that should be made to the cafeteria or the school vending machines are _____.

5. Changes that should be made on our school buses are _____.

6. School uniforms should (or should not) be required.

© 2005 Englefield & Associates, Inc.

6 Additional Resources

The following titles will provide support for additional sources of models for each of the communication processes. You may want to utilize selections with your students to examine the features of the communication process as a reading or "read aloud" selection, or you may use an individual title in its entirety for classroom study. The model lesson from *Write on Target* can be paired with the appropriate graphic organizer and a model from the text for an easy-to-plan writing lesson. This list of titles is not meant to be comprehensive; you can add to the list with materials from your own classroom.

Titles to Support the Narrative Communication Process

Bledsoe, Lucy Jane	Cougar Canyon
Byars, Betsy	My Dog, My Hero
Cameron, Ann	The Stories Julian Tells
Dahl, Roald	The BFG
DeLaCroix, Alice	The Hero of Third Grade
Ferris, Jeri	Go Free or Die: A Story About Harriet Tubman
Goodman, Susan E.	Robert Heny Hendershot
Jeffers, Susan	Brother Eagle, Sister Sky: A Message from Chief Seattle
Lowry, Lois	Gooney Bird Greene
Polacco, Patricia	The Keeping Quilt
Quattlebaum, Mary	Jackson Jones and the Puddle of Thorns
Robinson, Barbara	The Best School Year Ever
Sadler, Marilyn	Stuck on Earth
Scieszka, Jon	Squids Will Be Squids
White, E. B.	Charlotte's Web

Titles to Support the Descriptive Communication Process

Brenner, Barbara	One Small Place in a Tree
Cronin, Doreen	Diary of a Worm
Dadey, Debbie and	
Jones, Marcia Thornton	Vampires Don't Wear Polka Dots
DuPrau, Jeanne	The City of Ember
Griffith, Helen V.	Caitlin's Holiday
Jenkins, Steve	Actual Size
Kline, Suzy	Horrible Harry Moves Up to Third Grade
Myers, Laurie	Earthquake in the Third Grade
Pinkney, Andrea D.	Bill Pickett: Rodeo-Ridin' Cowboy
Stowe, Cynthia	Not-So-Normal Norman

Titles to Support the Direction Communication Process

Duffey, Betsy	How to Be Cool in the Third Grade
Goodman, Susan E.	On This Spot: An Expedition Back Through Time
Krull, Kathleen	The Boy on Fairfield Street: How Ted Geisel Grew Up to Become Dr. Seuss
Paulson, Gary	How Angel Peterson Got His Name
Rockwell, Thomas	How to Eat Fried Worms
Rylant, Cynthia	In Aunt Lucy's Kitchen
Schyffert, Bea Uusma	The Man Who Went to the Far Side of the Moon: The Story of Apollo 11 Astronaut Michael Collins

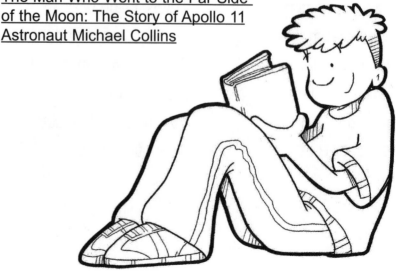

Titles to Support the Explanation Communication Process

Anderson, Laurie Halse	Thank You, Sarah: The Woman Who Saved Thanksgiving
Burleigh, Robert	Langston's Train Ride
Duffey, Betsy	The Gadget War
Krull, Kathleen	Harvesting Hope: The Story of Cesar Chavez
Lisle, Janet Taylor	The Gold Dust Letters
Miller, Debbie S.	Arctic Lights, Arctic Nights
Naden, Corinne J.	Dian Fossey: At Home With the Giant Gorillas
Osborne, Mary Pope	Dolphins and Sharks (Magic Tree House Research Guide Series)
Rossiter, Nan Parson	Sugar on Snow
Rumford, James	Sequoyah: The Cherokee Man Who Gave His People Writing
Wick, Walter	Walter Wick's Optical Tricks
Winkler, Henry	Niagra Falls, Or Does It? (Hank Zipzer #1)

Titles to Support the Persuasive Communication Process

Allie, Debora	The Meanest Girl
Bruchac, Joseph	A Boy Called Slow
Chetwin, Grade	Friend in Time
Golenbock, Peter	Teammates
McKenna, Colleen O'Shaughnessy	Good Grief . . . Third Grade
Philbrick, Rodman	Write a Book Review
Waggoner, Karen	Partners

Teacher Notes

Teacher Notes

Teacher Notes

Teacher Notes

Subject-Specific Skill Development
Workbooks Increase Testing Skills

Write on Target
for grades 1/2,
3, 4, 5, and 6

Includes
Graphic Organizers

Read on Target
for grades 1/2,
3, 4, 5, and 6

Includes
Reading Maps

Math on Target for grades 3, 4, and 5

Includes Thinking Maps

For more information, call our toll-free number: 1.877.PASSING (727.7464)
or visit our website: www.showwhatyouknowpublishing.com